THE BEST IS YET TO BE

"The midlife years can really be surprisingly tough ones. But my friend, Bruce Peppin, does a great job in guiding us through the challenges we face and inspires us to finish strong."

Dr. Kevin Leman, author of *Have a Happy Family by Friday*

"If you live to be eighty-two, you only have 20,000 days to live your life. How will you spend your days? Bruce Peppin's book will cause you to ask hard questions and lead you on the path to finish your days well. Read this book, it could change your life!"

Linda Dillow, author of *What's It Like to Be Married to Me?*

"I love how Bruce brings depth to his ultimate optimism through biblical principles and life experiences—and how his practical strategies for finishing well makes me actually look *forward* to getting older!"

Cynthia Tobias, author of *The Way They Learn*

"I highly recommend this book. *The Best Is Yet to Be* is an excellent and practical resource. I found this message inspiring and was filled with passion for the days that are yet ahead of me."

Tom Doyle, vice president of e3 Partners and author of *Dreams and Visions*

"What a timely reminder Bruce has given us as we continue to run the race. Like a writer who needs to keep his pencil sharpened, we need to sharpen our focus, commitment, and resolve. What a joy it is to join in with my own recommitment to finishing strong."

Lynda Hunter Bjorklund, EdD, author, speaker, and founding editor of Focus on the Family's *Single-Parent Family* magazine

THE
BEST IS
YET TO BE

MOVING MOUNTAINS
IN MIDLIFE

BRUCE PEPPIN

David C Cook®
transforming lives together

THE BEST IS YET TO BE
Published by David C Cook
4050 Lee Vance View
Colorado Springs, CO 80918 U.S.A.

David C Cook Distribution Canada
55 Woodslee Avenue, Paris, Ontario, Canada N3L 3E5

David C Cook U.K., Kingsway Communications
Eastbourne, East Sussex BN23 6NT, England

The graphic circle C logo is a registered trademark of David C Cook.

The website addresses recommended throughout this book are offered as a
resource to you. These websites are not intended in any way to be or imply an
endorsement on the part of David C Cook, nor do we vouch for their content.

Unless otherwise noted, all Scripture quotations are taken from the New American
Standard Bible®, Copyright © 1960, 1995 by The Lockman Foundation. Used
by permission. (www.Lockman.org.) Scripture quotations marked MSG are taken
from THE MESSAGE. Copyright © by Eugene H. Peterson 1993, 2002. Used
by permission of NavPress Publishing Group; NIV are taken from the Holy Bible,
New International Version®, NIV®. Copyright © 1973, 2011 by Biblica, Inc.™
Used by permission of Zondervan. All rights reserved worldwide. www.zondervan.
com; and NLT are taken from the *Holy Bible*, New Living Translation, copyright
© 1996, 2007 by Tyndale House Foundation. Used by permission of Tyndale
House Publishers, Inc., Carol Stream, Illinois 60188. All rights reserved.

Some names have been changed to protect individuals and their stories.

LCCN 2014948801
ISBN 978-0-7814-1104-2
eISBN 978-1-4347-0901-1

© 2015 Bruce D. Peppin
The Team: Alex Field, Ingrid Beck, Traci DePree,
Nick Lee, Tiffany Thomas, Karen Athen
Cover Design: Amy Konyndyk
Cover Photo: iStockphoto

Printed in the United States of America
First Edition 2015

1 2 3 4 5 6 7 8 9 10

120314

To my wife, Kathleen,
my son and daughter-in-law, Brooks and Jordyn,
and my daughter, Brianna.
Each has been an inspiration for this book
and is on the journey with me to finish life well.

CONTENTS

FOREWORD

Back when I was a boy, every television show or movie portraying a man in the throes of a midlife crisis seemed to follow a similar script. The character, usually a balding, slightly overweight individual, appears frustrated and often bored with life. At some point, he's seen holding a drink, taking a long draw on a cigarette or cigar, and gazing longingly out to the horizon. For some reason, the man is often standing alone and along the ocean's edge. His life hasn't unfolded according to plan. The dreams of his youth are now dashed. He feels "stuck"—stuck in a job, stuck in a relationship, and stuck trying to manage the mundane minutiae of everyday life.

So, what does he do?

Inevitably, he decides to shake free from the shackles of convention. The antidote to the malaise is adventure, but often of the selfish sort. Soon, the character is seen driving a red convertible down an open road with a beautiful blonde by his side. Or maybe we see him lying on a beach in some exotic locale.

The subtle but clear message is this: true liberation in life can be achieved only if we focus on ourselves. The so-called "straight" life is a boorish burden. Traditional milestones—finishing school, getting married, having children, coaching youth sports, volunteering at your church, and focusing on others—might be all right for some, but not for those who really want to experience the *good* life.

Of course, what the screenwriters don't always show us is all the brokenness behind those who pursue the sports car or the extramarital affair. We rarely see the first wife (or the ex-wife) or the children waiting for Dad to come to his senses—and come home—instead of going to a bar with the boys. The result of this selfish pursuit is at best a quiet desperation and, at worst, a complete disaster.

It doesn't have to be that way.

At least the apostle Paul didn't think so. As he approached the end of his earthly ministry, Paul was able to say, "I have fought the good fight, I have finished the race, I have kept the faith" (2 Tim. 4:7 NIV). He never abandoned his principles. He never wavered from the course. And when it came time to cross the finish line, he did so with contentment and joy.

How did he do it? Can we follow in Paul's footsteps? My friend Bruce Peppin believes you can. So strongly does he believe this, in fact, that he's written this book to help you make it happen. *The Best Is Yet to Be: Moving Mountains in Midlife* is a reflection of the author's love for people and his passion to equip, enable, and encourage his fellow believers to *finish well.* Bruce himself is pursuing this challenge, and he wants to take as many others along for the ride as he possibly can.

I've been acquainted with Bruce long enough—more than two decades—to know that he knows his stuff. Even more importantly, I can testify to the solidity of his commitment to Jesus Christ. He has a gentle but tenacious spirit, a calm and steady temperament, a genuine gift for leadership, and an ability to discern God's truth clearly in the darkest and most confusing of circumstances. So firm is his dedication to the work of the kingdom that he has for many years been part of a group that walks the halls of Focus on the Family headquarters during the early morning hours simply in order to pray for the staff before the day begins. If anyone understands what it means to follow Christ with integrity and courage, it's Bruce Peppin.

Now that I'm in my fifties, Bruce's charge in the following pages is personal to me. Like you, I'm committed to dedicating the remainder of my life to doing significant work. I've been blessed to spend the last quarter century at Focus on the Family, and never before in the history of the ministry have we been helping more people. But you don't have to be working full-time in Christian ministry to make a difference and contribute in a significant way. All of us are called to play our part.

When the eighteenth-century preacher Jonathan Edwards was just eighteen years of age, he preached his first sermon. His main thesis was that Christians should be a happy people, not downcast or heavy burdened. He gave three reasons why:

1. Our bad things will turn out for good.
2. Our good things can never be taken away from us.
3. *The best things are yet to come.*

What mountains are you trying to move in your life? I realize that some folks believe our current situation has grown pretty bleak, but from where I sit, it's an exciting time to be alive. God is great, and He has lots of big, important things for each and every one of us to do in His service! That's why I'm so enthusiastic about tomorrow. If you agree—or if you're looking for something that will help you catch this vision—I highly recommend that you turn the page and find out what Bruce has to say on the subject.

And like Jonathan Edwards suggested and God's Word affirms, the best really *is* yet to come!

Jim Daly
President and CEO of Focus on the Family

ACKNOWLEDGMENTS

Grateful. That is how I feel toward God and everyone who helped make this book a reality.

My wife, Kathleen, has lived through its pages, which was no small task. I am thankful to have journeyed with her for over thirty-one years.

I am indebted to Tim and Diane Jones and my home group that threw down the gauntlet one evening telling me that I needed to pursue the stirrings of my heart—to help others finish life well. They encouraged me to get serious about what I thought the Lord was leading me to do. When I needed some time away, Tim took me out into the wilderness to climb some of Colorado's fourteen-thousand-foot mountains. In the beauty of that backcountry and through the companionship of a close friend, I found my heart spiritually refreshed.

I've lost count of how many divine appointments took place during the many conversations I had with my friend and colleague Ron Wilson. His spiritual insights and counsel have been life changing.

Nearly every day, Chris Perez asked how my book writing was going. He often told me, "If you don't write this book, God will raise up someone else who will!" That was convicting and kept me pressing ahead when momentum slowed.

Tom Doyle, my pastor and friend, was a big supporter of this project. He introduced me to an experienced agent, David R. Shepherd. I was honored when David agreed to represent my book, and I appreciated his wise coaching along the way.

This book was enriched by the wisdom of Jody and Linda Dillow, Tony and Becky Metcalf, Brad and Meshell Watt, Tom and JoAnn Doyle, David Brown, Denny Repko, Jim Downing, Chris Crossan, Gene Ashe,

Jack Boghosian, Jacki Kintz, Lon Adams, Paul Batura, and Ray Vander Laan. Others have remained anonymous, but they shared stories that underscored the importance of finishing well in life.

I remember the day I found out that David C Cook wanted to publish my book. I was overwhelmed with the sense of God's favor on this endeavor. David C Cook has brought many outstanding titles to the market. I hope this is another one! I want to express my gratitude to Alex Field and his exceptional team for all their efforts in producing and promoting the book you now hold in your hands. Amy Konyndyk created an amazing cover and worked hard to get it just right. I took to heart Traci DePree's probing questions and editorial recommendations, which significantly improved the manuscript.

I am also grateful for you, the reader, who will be turning the following pages. You will quickly know the value of this book's message in your life and whether others should be told about it. My prayer is that both will be the case.

INTRODUCTION

I hit a wall in May 2000. I didn't know if my marriage was going to make it or if I could hold my family together. Most of all, I felt betrayed and abandoned by God. The irony was I worked for a Christian ministry.

I felt like a phony, just going through the motions while my life was falling apart. Depression had me by the throat, and I couldn't pull out of its grip.

I left work for a month. During this time, I met with a psychiatrist, traveled with my wife, Kathleen, to reconnect, hiked in the Rocky Mountains, and used the time away to regroup.

Upon reflection, there were many lessons I learned by going through that crisis. The biggest one was realizing I had been trying to live life on my own terms. I was defining the ground rules and determining how I should measure success and happiness. That approach lasted for a while, given my high degree of effort and control. But at some point, life didn't fit within a comfortable box. More doubts began to spill out, and soon it felt as though the floodgates had opened.

There are many unknowns when a decision is made to change direction and live life according to *God's terms*. When Jesus called Levi, a tax collector, He said only two words: "Follow Me!" (Mark 2:14). There were no explanations or guarantees of what life would be like. Jesus was simply telling him, "Trust Me; I know the way." After wrestling with what to do, I chose to follow Him without having all the answers.

My feelings of abandonment by God diminished and eventually gave way to a growing sense of connection to Him. My problems didn't all go away, but I handled them much differently than before. It was no longer a mentality that said, "If I do this, then, God, You're obligated to do that." There was no more performing or trying to earn God's favor.

Those were my old terms, and I cast them aside. Now I could embrace the Lord of heaven who knew me by name and promised to lead the way even when I couldn't see where the path was going.

I realize what I am saying might seem like a spiritual leap to some people. It's possible you may feel far away from God, as I did, or not even know if God is there. That is totally understandable. It is a core issue we must grapple with in life. For readers who may be interested, I have written a section (appendix A in the back of this book) about what a personal relationship with the Lord looks like. Or perhaps you're a follower of Jesus but have grown weary and discouraged. I am hoping the topics discussed and the help offered in this book will provide a needed boost to your faith.

The title of my book, *The Best Is Yet to Be*, emphasizes the point that there is genuine hope for our future even though the obstacles confronting us may seem like mountains blocking our way. I am encouraged to read what Jesus told His disciples about these kinds of mountains: "For truly I say to you, if you have faith the size of a mustard seed, you will say to this mountain, 'Move from here to there,' and it will move; and nothing will be impossible to you" (Matt. 17:20). The subtitle, *Moving Mountains in Midlife*, is based on this amazing promise and will be explored in the pages ahead.

What we're after is a life that knows God personally and experiences Him moving the mountains for us. There is no secret formula to it; only proven biblical priorities and principles can guide us along the right path. Jesus described it like this: "Enter through the narrow gate; for the gate is wide and the way is broad that leads to destruction, and there are many who enter through it. For the gate is small and the way is narrow that leads to life, and there are few who find it" (Matt. 7:13–14). It is important to remember that Jesus is both the gate we are to enter by and the way we are to travel on. He is the key to everything!

By keeping on that narrow way, we will chart the course to arrive at our ultimate destination—heaven! Until then, this daily journey can also be called "pursuing a life that finishes well for the Lord." It is an essential idea that we will discuss at some length.

The years after I hit the wall were spent doing a deep dive into the Scriptures, trying to make sense out of all the crises I had faced. One area that needed adjusting was my understanding about who God really is and the intense love He has for us. To our own detriment, we dismiss the incredible majesty of our Creator. Whether we realize it or not, the Almighty is our greatest ally. But there is also an Enemy of our souls who is just as real. While we need not fear him, we must understand his tactics and use the weapons God has placed in our hands to defeat him.

I have come to believe that the territories of our minds are where the most significant battles on earth take place. It is here that the Enemy stands against us and the work of God in our hearts. Winning the battle of the mind can dramatically alter our lives and the legacy we leave to future generations. This lesson was driven home to me very directly (which I will talk about in coming chapters).

Being optimistic that the best is yet to be, seeing mountains moved, and finishing well for the Lord all tie together. I should point out, though, that this book is not the final word on these topics by any means. I certainly have not arrived and am still in the trenches like everyone else. In fact, I struggled with whether I was qualified to write this book because of my own shortcomings and the daunting scope of the material.

I took heart in knowing that God is the mountain mover and has already determined what characterizes a life that finishes well. He loves for us to search out His principles in the Scriptures and present them for others to examine. That is what I have attempted to do.

I organized the book into five sections and then included appendixes with additional information. Each section builds on the previous one, but you are welcome to jump to any part that interests you. You'll notice that I have incorporated photos, paintings, poetry, quotations, and many stories to illustrate the principles given.

At the end of each chapter is a word of encouragement called a Moving Mountains Moment. These are meant to inspire you that God can move the highest mountain on your behalf.

The last section includes discussion and Bible study questions for each chapter. This will take you deeper into the content. It is designed for personal or group use.

I present a definition of what a life that finishes well looks like for your consideration. It is based on the two great commandments of Jesus—first, to love God; and second, to love your neighbor as yourself (Matt. 22:37–39). I hope it inspires you to write your own definition! Because I am a visual learner, I developed a graphic design that shows how all the priorities and principles of the book connect together. You can find it on page 283.

I also want to emphasize that experiencing the kind of life I'm describing here is possible for *everyone*. No one is excluded because of past or present failures. No one is beyond God's reach or His love.

Jesus shared a remarkable parable about the kingdom of heaven that relates to this idea of not being excluded from God's love because of past or present failings. You can read the story in Matthew 20:1–16.

It goes like this: A landowner hired laborers early in the morning to work in his vineyard. He offered to pay them a day's wage, which they were happy to receive. The landowner hired additional laborers throughout the day, even until five o'clock in the evening. Shortly after the final hires, it was time to quit and he called the workers together. He paid each one a full day's wage. This bothered those who had started early in the morning even though they received the amount they had agreed to. Jesus used this teaching to give an example of what God's generosity looks like. It has nothing to do with the worker's efforts but is entirely dependent on the landowner's—God's—benevolence.

This holds true in our relationship with Jesus as we seek to finish well. Regardless of age or how far away we may have wandered, as long as we have breath, we can still return and answer His invitation to "Follow Me."

Then someday won't it be wonderful to hear those incredible words from the Lord: "Well done, good and faithful servant!" (Matt. 25:21 NIV)? The following pages will help guide us toward that destination.

I look forward to joining you on the journey!

Bruce Peppin
Colorado Springs, Colorado

PART ONE

THE CHALLENGE

Scouting the Territory for Moving Mountains

1

LIFE IN REVIEW

The Great Pyramid of Giza is a stunning sight. The immensity of its size is overwhelming and its architecture brilliant. It was built around 2560 BC as the burial place for Pharaoh Khufu. As one of the Seven Wonders of the Ancient World, it rose over 480 feet from the desert floor with sides spanning about 750 feet at the base. It was the tallest structure known to man for nearly four millennia. Yet, in an irony of history, the only surviving statue of Khufu is an insignificant ivory sculpture three inches tall.

Domitian, the Roman emperor (AD 81–96), demanded that he be addressed as "Lord and God" and worshipped as deity. Refusing to do so meant a brutal death. To honor Domitian, the city of Ephesus built a large temple that housed a massive marble statue of his image. Eventually, members of his inner court assassinated him by stabbing him repeatedly with a dagger. Today all that is left of his pompous effigy is a marred and cracked head with part of a left arm. His temple lies in ruins, stones scattered around a few decrepit walls and columns. Not much to show for someone who claimed to be divine.

In the late nineteenth and early twentieth centuries, Henry Huntington made millions as a railroad and real estate tycoon. He built a fifty-five-thousand-square-foot French-style villa in San Marino, California, in 1911. His wife, Arabella, was the wealthiest woman in America. While Henry collected rare books and art, Arabella spent vast fortunes on jewelry. Her private collection was one of the world's most prestigious at the time, mainly purchased from Parisian jewelers, including Cartier.

After Arabella's death in 1924, the treasure trove of jewels went to her son, Archer, and his wife, Anna. The pair did not share Arabella's appreciation for precious stones and sold the whole collection to a young jeweler named Harry Winston. Winston removed the gems from their old-fashioned settings, then recut and sold them across the world. He boasted that Arabella's famous seven-strand, 497-pearl necklace adorned the necks of over two dozen women.

History books are filled with the storied lives of pharaohs, emperors, tycoons, and heiresses who sought fame and fortune, hoping to create a lasting legacy. Most spent their years on vain endeavors, leaving the world without discovering a treasure greater than anything gained on earth—a relationship with the God of heaven.

Thousands of years before, King Solomon observed this pattern and said, "I hated all the fruit of my labor for which I had labored under the sun, for I must leave it to the man who will come after me" (Eccles. 2:18). He then summarized it all by saying, "The conclusion, when all has been heard, is: fear God and keep His commandments, because this applies to every person" (Eccles. 12:13).

The concluding advice from the wisest and wealthiest man in the world doesn't exhort us to seek more possessions, prestige, or earthly pursuits. He must have surprised his readers when he pointed them to God as the ultimate prize for life.

Another way Solomon might have expressed his counsel would be, "Invest your life in what has eternal value! True treasure is found in knowing God and living fully for Him." This is the kind of life that finishes well for the Lord.

Mark Twain's View of Life

The great writer Mark Twain struggled to find meaning in life after losing his twenty-four-year-old daughter, Susy, to spinal meningitis. Years later, he wrote about her death in his autobiography and described his opinion of human existence this way:

A myriad of men are born; they labor and sweat and struggle for bread; they squabble and scold and fight; they scramble for little mean advantages over each other; age creeps upon them; infirmities follow; shames and humiliations bring down their prides and their vanities; those they love are taken from them, and the joy of life is turned to aching grief. The burden of pain, care, misery, grows heavier year by year; at length ambition is dead; pride is dead; vanity is dead; longing for release is in their place. It comes at last—the only unpoisoned gift earth ever had for them—and they vanish from a world where they were of no consequence; where they achieved nothing; where they were a mistake and a failure and a foolishness; where they have left no sign that they have existed—a world which will lament them a day and forget them forever.[1]

Few people can articulate the human condition as well as he did. His words cut to the core and leave us questioning if they might be true of our lives. Are we of no consequence? Will we vanish and leave no mark? Are we like every pharaoh, emperor, and wealthy heiress who puts his or her trust in the wrong things only to see them slip away at death? Is this how our lives will turn out?

The answer to these questions for someone who seeks to follow the Lord is a definite *no*! At the same time, we also acknowledge the reality of life that Twain described as "the burden of pain, care, misery [that] grows heavier year by year." We don't discount the gravity of our circumstances. Instead, we draw a different conclusion concerning where they lead us.

Mother Teresa received the Nobel Peace Prize in 1979 for her humanitarian efforts. All lauded the invaluable work of the Missionaries of Charity in Calcutta, India. At less than five feet tall, this diminutive woman had a commanding presence before world leaders who heard her pleas on behalf of the poor and disabled. However, when out of the public eye, she struggled with feelings of inner darkness and emotional pain in her longing for God. It was a lifelong battle. She shared those burdens only with her superiors.

Here is an excerpt from a letter she wrote to Father Neuner, one of her spiritual advisers, in her unique style of writing:

Now Father—since [1949 or 1950] this terrible sense of loss—this untold darkness—this loneliness—this continual longing for God—which gives me that pain deep down in my heart.—Darkness is such that I really do not see— neither with my mind nor with my reason...—Sometimes—I just hear my own heart cry out—"My God" and nothing else comes.—The torture and pain I can't explain....

You see, Father, the contradiction in my life. I long for God—I want to love Him—to love Him much—to live only for love of Him—to love only—and yet there is but pain—longing and no love....

Yet deep down somewhere in my heart that longing for God keeps breaking through the darkness.[2]

Are you surprised to hear these words coming from someone like Mother Teresa? She is not diminished in my eyes because she wrestled with her faith in God at such deep levels. It is actually encouraging to know she dealt with heavy burdens and came through them just as we can. She saw a break in the darkness that gave her hope for her spiritual struggles. Teresa requested that her letters be destroyed when she was gone, feeling they were too personal and might cause some to doubt their faith. Father Neuner realized how beneficial they would be for others to read and decided instead to preserve them.

The Brevity of Life

For those of us in our midlife years, it is shocking how quickly time has passed by. The memories of raising children, participating in countless birthday parties, trips to the emergency room, holiday gatherings, and school, church, and sporting events are still lodged in our minds. Who hit the fast-forward button that brought it all to a close and ushered in this new season of life?

Moses pondered how quickly a lifetime passes on the earth. In Psalm 90, he said:

> As for the days of our life, they contain seventy years,
>
> Or if due to strength, eighty years,
>
> Yet their pride is but labor and sorrow;
>
> For soon it is gone and we fly away....
>
> So teach us to number our days,
>
> That we may present to You a heart of wisdom. (vv. 10, 12)

At first glance, Moses might appear to lean toward Twain's assessment of life by emphasizing its brevity, labor, and sorrow. However, he quickly looked to God to fill his days with purpose. He hoped to someday possess a heart of wisdom that would honor the Lord's ways. At the end of his life, he had come very near to that goal.

From a stammering reluctance to follow God's command to free Israel from slavery, Moses went on to lead one of the most renowned lives in all the Scriptures. He successfully defeated the pharaoh of Egypt who stood as the world's tyrant. The Almighty used him to deliver the Jewish people from captivity and toward possession of a new land. Moses hand carried the law of God that has guided humanity for centuries. He was a prophet, leader, writer, judge, worker of wonders, and a friend of the Lord of Hosts. The book of Deuteronomy gives him a "finishing well" tribute:

> Since that time no prophet has risen in Israel like Moses,
> whom the LORD knew face to face, for all the signs and
> wonders which the LORD sent him to perform in the land of

Egypt against Pharaoh, all his servants, and all his land, and
for all the mighty power and for all the great terror which
Moses performed in the sight of all Israel. (34:10–12)

Think of what would have happened had Moses shrunk back in fear?
He would have missed out on being a part of some of the Lord's greatest
work in the history of mankind. Instead, he was able to overcome his
fears, and he found the Almighty more than adequate to compensate for
his shortcomings.

As Moses looked back over his life, he wrote about numbering his days
to stay focused on what was important. Following his example, if we lived to
be eighty-two years old, that would give us about thirty thousand days
to be alive. From there, we'd be awake approximately twenty thousand days
with the other ten thousand spent sleeping. Based on these summaries, I've
already used 70 percent of my allotment. How about you?

Baby Boomer Generation

As the largest generation in history, the baby boomers exploded onto the
scene following World War II with their ranks swelling to seventy-six
million between 1946 and 1964. They marched through the cultural
upheavals in the 1960s and 1970s, enjoyed economic prosperity, and
held an idealistic view of what society could become.

Given the favorable conditions that surrounded the baby boomers,
one might expect them to have an optimistic view of life. However,
studies conducted by the Pew Research Center discovered something
different. In the December 2010 Social and Demographic Trends report,
Pew stated:

> The iconic image of the Baby Boom generation is a 1960s-
> era snapshot of an exuberant, long-haired, rebellious young
> adult.... This famously huge cohort of Americans finds itself
> in a funk as it approaches old age....

Some of this pessimism is related to life cycle—for most people, middle age is the most demanding and stressful time of life. Some of the gloominess, however, appears to be particular to Boomers, who bounded onto the national stage in the 1960s with high hopes for remaking society, but who've spent most of their adulthood trailing other age cohorts in overall life satisfaction.[3]

While the findings describing baby boomers seem melancholy, this book offers a hopeful vision of what life can be like for those in midlife or nearby seasons. There are reasons for optimism that can transcend the pessimism so many in this life stage are characterized by.

Memories of a Mentor

Compare these findings to a man who chose to live differently—filled with purpose and inspiration for others—during the second half of his life. His name was Stan Reed. He served as a pastor in several congregations and earned a reputation as someone to call on if anyone had a need. By worldly standards, he did not earn much money or achieve earthly fame. Yet his influence touched the lives of thousands of people.

I received a phone call saying that Stan had passed away at his home in Southern California. I knew he was close to the end, but the finality of the news hit me hard.

A flood of memories swept over me. I was back at high school, sitting in his office where he told me about Jesus. During college he followed my progress with interest and suggested I consider entering the ministry. I later joined him on the church staff as a youth pastor.

Stan's family asked me to speak at his memorial service. In preparation I dug through some old boxes and found a small book that the youth of the church had given me on my twenty-fifth birthday over thirty-five years earlier.

As I thumbed through it, I came across a page where Stan had written his birthday wishes to me in his left-handed scrawl:

Dear Bruce,

I don't have long to write, but sometimes the shortest and deepest feelings are best received. You have been like a son to me and a good one. I will always cherish our friendship.

May God bless you real good.

With Brotherly Love in Christ,
Stan Reed
Prov. 3:5–6

I had forgotten he had written in that little book. I sat down and fought tears as the meaning of the words sank in again. They revealed the character of this godly, caring man who had taken the time to invest in a young person's life.

At Stan's memorial service, loved ones surrounded him. Connie (his wife of fifty-six years), his five children, fifteen grandchildren, three great-grandchildren, two brothers, sister, and hundreds of friends all came to honor him.

Here are some highlights of sentiments shared:

Steve said, "He was a good and faithful father to me and a faithful husband to my mom. He showed me a lot of grace, especially when I crashed the family car when I was in high school. When my first son was being born, I wondered where my dad was. I later found out he was counseling a couple in the hallway of the hospital and led them to the Lord."

Debra stated, "I'm proud to be the daughter of Stan Reed. He showed me unconditional love."

Janet shared a poem she had written that concluded with "Well done, good and faithful servant."

Susan and Nancy both sang songs.

As I listened to his children speak fondly about him, I wondered what mine would say about me someday.

Stan showed me that it was possible to finish well and leave a far-reaching legacy with our family and friends regardless of how society might measure success. He lived intuitively, from the heart born out of a deep faith in God.

Some of us, however, are going to need help setting the correct course in order to live a life that finishes well for the Lord. We can start right where we are. That is the purpose of this book.

The human condition Mark Twain described is one view of our earthly existence, but it does not need to define us. We can choose a different path. It will take grit and determined commitment to make that journey, but there is no greater endeavor to pursue.

Moving Mountains Moment

For many of us, the problems we face seem like impassable mountains. But there is hope! Jesus spent a lot of time telling people that mountains can be moved by His power. Do we believe Him? The saying "Don't measure the size of the mountain; talk to the One who can move it" emphasizes this idea. The following verse provides an encouraging reminder of what God can do as we seek Him for help: "Let every valley be lifted up, and every mountain and hill be made low; and let the rough ground become a plain, and the rugged terrain a broad valley" (Isa. 40:4).

Note: Near the end of this book, starting on page 247, you will find discussion and Bible study questions for each chapter. You can use these questions for personal or group study.

2

THE NARROW WAY

Depending on whom you ask, you'll receive varying opinions about what it means to finish well.

To a professional football player, winning the Super Bowl would be the measure. The same could be said for an actor accepting an Oscar or a soldier receiving the Medal of Honor.

Mother Teresa and Princess Diana died within days of each other in 1997. Diana was thirty-six when she died on August 31, and Mother Teresa was eighty-seven, dying on September 5. These two women inspired the world with their humanitarian efforts.

Diana had visited Mother Teresa in New York on June 18 of that year. No one could have imagined they would both be dead less than three months later. Their hearts for the downtrodden may have been similar, but their lives were lived in stark contrast.

One felt called to serve the poor on the streets of Calcutta, shunning wealth and power. The other also had a heart for the outcast, but she used the influence of royalty and wealth to bring about change.

When the tragic news of Diana's death became public, the media focused on little else. It was 24-7

Mother Teresa and Princess Diana (Alpha Photo Press Ltd., London, used with permission)

coverage for weeks. Every aspect of her life was analyzed and her philan-
thropy extolled. Britain's population went into national mourning, joined
by people from around the globe.

Five days later the world said good-bye to another exceptional woman
whose list of accomplishments were arguably far greater than Diana's.
While Mother Teresa's passing barely caught the attention of the media,
it did provide an interesting counterpoint to the loss of the former
Princess of Wales.

Judging from the media attention, there was no question that Diana's
life was regarded as the more acclaimed. However, of all the candidates in
Gallup's Eighteen Most Admired People of the Century, Mother Teresa
placed at the number one spot above every president, celebrity, and
humanitarian.[1] Does that surprise you? Her example of self-sacrifice in
caring for the poor was so compelling that it influenced the entire world
to rethink what was truly important.

As we look back on the lives of these remarkable women, how do we
evaluate the legacy they left? The answer depends on our standard of measure.

Heaven's Weights and Measures

The words recorded in Revelation 20:11–12 indicate that heaven has its
own set of "weights and measures" that will be used to judge mankind
and angels. A life registered on these scales will score much differently
than on our temporal ones.

Here is how Scripture describes it:

> Then I saw a great white throne and Him who sat upon it,
> from whose presence earth and heaven fled away, and no place
> was found for them. And I saw the dead, the great and the
> small, standing before the throne, and books were opened;
> and another book was opened, which is the book of life; and

the dead were judged from the things which were written in
the books, according to their deeds.

This passage recounts the final judgment. God will render His ultimate verdict that carries infinite consequences for each of us. No one
should stand in that moment wondering what might happen!

Being confident that we gave our hearts to Jesus, accepting His payment on the cross for the price of our sins, will make that event a joyous
homecoming filled with commendation and rewards. Something so
important must not be left to chance. It requires deliberate action on our
part to follow the narrow way laid out in the biblical text.

Finding Our Path

How do we find that path? What are the divine instructions? While it
might appear to be straightforward to read the counsel of the Scriptures
and follow the advice given, it can often be surprisingly difficult in application. Climbing my first fourteen-thousand-foot mountain in Colorado
is a case in point.

Uncompahgre Peak (T. Duren Jones, used with permission)

Uncompahgre Peak rises to 14,309 feet and is the highest summit in the San Juan Mountains located in southwestern Colorado. At the invitation of my friend Tim Jones, I joined him on this high-altitude trek. As an experienced mountaineer, he outfitted us with the appropriate gear and maps. However, I quickly learned that in the wilderness, trails are not always easy to follow, even when you have a map.

We left at sunrise and were mesmerized by the beauty of the pristine landscape. Gradually, the trail became steeper and more barren. We halted at a spot where the path diverged in a couple of directions. After checking our map, we chose to go right and then headed up the mountain.

Nearly an hour passed and we didn't seem to be getting any closer to our destination. Looking across the valley, we saw the hulking form of the peak in the distance. Pulling the map out again, it was clear we had chosen the wrong trail.

How can you miss a 14,309-foot mountain looming right in front of you? We sheepishly admitted our error and tracked back down the way we had come. Returning to the junction of trails, we chose the other path and eventually arrived at the summit.

The life lesson was clear. If I can miss a gigantic mountain standing in front of me, what else am I liable to miss—maybe living a life that finishes well? It was certainly a topic of conversation for the rest of the trip.

Two Verses about Finishing Well

Many verses in the Bible relate to finishing well. Among them, two rise up above the rest: Matthew 22, verses 37 and 39. They were spoken by Jesus in response to a lawyer who tested Him by asking what the greatest commandment was.

When the crowd heard the lawyer's question, they knew a cunning trap lay behind his seemingly innocent words. A note in the NLT Study Bible says, "Since many strict Jews saw all the commandments as equally binding, a careless response to this question could lead to the accusation of undermining the law of God."[2] Everyone leaned in to hear how Jesus would respond. He replied by quoting Scripture:

> "You shall love the LORD your God with all your heart, and with all your soul, and with all your mind." This is the great and foremost commandment. The second is like it, "You shall love your neighbor as yourself." On these two commandments depend the whole Law and the Prophets. (vv. 37–40)

The lawyer must have stood slack jawed hearing this authoritative answer that turned his understanding of the Law on its head. His trap had utterly failed. It is significant to note that Jesus was quoting from Deuteronomy 6:5, which was part of the Shema, which all the Jewish people repeated in their daily prayers. The reference to loving your neighbor as yourself was not found in Deuteronomy, but in Leviticus 19:18. Jesus was the first to combine these texts summarizing the "whole Law and the Prophets," meaning the entire Old Testament, into two great commandments.

When we consider the kind of life that finishes well for the Lord, it makes sense to place these verses at the center of our conversation because they were pivotal teachings of Jesus. The psalmist wrote, "Your word is a lamp to my feet and a light to my path" (Ps. 119:105). In the same way, these two great commands can illuminate our path on this important journey.

If you were asked to define what finishing well means to you, what would you say? I know it's a big question, but jot down a few thoughts, if you can, in the following space.

_____

_____

_____

_____

Let's try to understand what the two great commands of Jesus really meant. First, what does it mean to love God? I realize whole books have been written about this, but here are some of my thoughts. See what you think.

With rare exception, if you love someone, you are in a relationship with him or her. Love and relationship go together. Typically, it's with family members and friends, but coworkers could also fit here. An emotional connection runs deep between you. You know what is important to them. You spend time with them. You're there when they need you. They are a priority to you. If you say you love someone but don't express it in tangible ways, is it genuine?

When Jesus described what our relationship to God should be like, He used the strong words of a lover. Does that surprise you? Your love is to be so close that *all your heart*—the very essence of who you are—is fully given to Him. Nothing is held back. So close that *all your soul*—your inner emotions and passions—are to be bound together with Him. So close that *all your mind*—your intellect and the thoughts that consume your daily life—are to be devoted entirely to Him. You are entreated by the God of the universe to enter into a love relationship with Him. The magnitude of that invitation is impossible to fully calculate. Yet it is there waiting for your response. How will you answer?

I am convinced that a life cannot finish well apart from having a personal relationship with our Creator. Jesus declared that loving God (really knowing Him) was the greatest commandment of all and most important for us to come to grips with. This is the first step we need to take on our journey to finish well in life. (As noted before, I explain what it means to have a personal relationship with God in appendix A.)

Another quality that characterizes loving God in our lives is found in John 17, which is an extraordinary chapter that reveals an intimate conversation and prayer that Jesus had with God the Father just before His arrest and crucifixion.

In the prayer, Jesus looked up to heaven and poured out His heart. He summarized His years of ministry by saying the grand purpose of why He came to earth was to give eternal life. He said, "Father, the hour has come; glorify Your Son, that the Son may glorify You, even as You gave Him authority over all flesh, that to all whom You have given Him, He may give eternal life" (John 17:1–2).

And then Jesus further expressed how He loved God: "I glorified You on the earth, having accomplished the work which You have given Me to do" (John 17:4).

What an amazing statement to declare! While every action Jesus took was to bring glory to God, He also did it out of profound love. His whole life was a vivid image of living out the first great commandment—to love God with all your heart, soul, and mind.

Likewise, we can show our love to God by serving Him through the work He calls us to do. However, at the end of our lives, we won't be able to say we accomplished everything. Only Jesus, who was God incarnate, can make that claim. The rest of us will need to admit our imperfect humanity and rely totally on God's strength for help in carrying out the work He assigns.

Think about that for a minute.

You and I have assignments coming from the throne of God to accomplish during our time on earth! These jobs have our names written on them; they are handpicked by God to enable us to strengthen the church and represent Him well to the world. As we do this, God is glorified through our lives.

Don't worry if you look around and aren't sure what God has assigned to you. It may not be evident at the moment, but it will unfold over time as you continue to walk with the Lord. Here is how the apostle Paul explained it: "For we are His workmanship, created in Christ Jesus for good works, which God prepared beforehand so that we would walk in them" (Eph. 2:10). God is ready to go. Are we?

Assignments from heaven will be as varied as the people who receive them. Sometimes we will recognize them when they arrive, and on other occasions we won't. Their significance isn't scalable. We must be careful not to think bigger is always better or more important. The opposite is frequently the case. Jesus had to remind His disciples, "The greatest among you shall be your servant. Whoever exalts himself shall be humbled; and whoever humbles himself shall be exalted" (Matt. 23:11–12).

If we are open to God's direction, we can be certain He will use our lives for His purposes in ways we can't imagine. This was true for a man who joined the Union army to fight in the Civil War. He didn't realize he was heading into a divine assignment. Have you heard about Joshua Chamberlain?

Joshua Chamberlain's Assignment

Joshua Chamberlain (1828–1914) was a thirty-three-year-old college professor at the outbreak of the Civil War. He enlisted in 1862 with the Union army and was assigned to the Twentieth Maine Regiment as a lieutenant colonel. He did not have prior military experience or training.

His regiment was sent to help defend Gettysburg, which was under attack by General Lee's army. On July 2, 1863, Chamberlain was ordered to hold a hill called Little Round Top at all costs. It represented the far left flank of the Union line and controlled a vital position in the battle.

The Fifteenth and Forty-Seventh Alabama Regiments repeatedly charged up the hillside to try to gain control of that all-important spot. Chamberlain's forces repelled them at considerable loss, dropping from three hundred men to a mere eighty, until their ammunition ran out. The troops were waiting to hear the order for retreat when, instead, they heard Chamberlain cry out, "Fix bayonets!" They were directed to engage in hand-to-hand combat rather than fall back.

Chamberlain led the charge down the hill, and in the midst of the chaos, the Confederates thought Union reinforcements had arrived. They broke rank and tried to escape. The Twentieth Maine Regiment captured more than one hundred enemy soldiers and secured one of the decisive victories of the Civil War. For his gallantry at Little Round Top, Chamberlain was awarded the Medal of Honor. He was later asked to preside over General Lee's surrender ceremony on April 9, 1865, at the Appomattox Court House.

Joshua Chamberlain could never have imagined what the divine assignment for his life would entail. He had no way to comprehend that he possessed such great courage until he was tested by the trials of combat. And he could not have foreseen that the victory he helped achieve on Little Round Top would add to the momentum that would ultimately result in the Union army's final triumph in the war.

While one of our assignments may not include fighting in a battle, we are already doing some of them without realizing it. For example, being a nurturing spouse or parent is high up on heaven's assignment list, as is being a faithful follower of Jesus. Beyond these, there is no end to the number of assignments that can come our way.

From what we have discussed about the first commandment of Jesus, loving God includes serving Him in the assignments He gives us. We also know it involves being in a close and connected relationship with Him.

Love My (Muslim?) Neighbor

Let's turn our attention to better understand the second great commandment—love your neighbor as yourself. This was a shocking statement for the time. Jesus removed the class distinctions that were rampant in the culture. To Jesus, everyone was worthy of love and should be treated with dignity, respect, and esteem. That includes those not in our group of friends.

"Loving our neighbor" was the topic of another lawyer's confrontation of Jesus:

> And a lawyer stood up and put Him to the test, saying, "Teacher, what shall I do to inherit eternal life?" And He said to him, "What is written in the Law? How does it read to you?" And he answered, "You shall love the LORD your God with all your heart, and with all your soul, and with all your strength, and with all your mind; and your neighbor as yourself." And He said to him, "You have answered correctly; do this and you will live." But wishing to justify himself, he said to Jesus, "And who is my neighbor?" (Luke 10:25–29)

Jesus then told him a story about a man who was robbed and badly beaten and left by the side of the road to die. Samaritans were despised by the Jews because of their mixed race with the Gentiles and different worship practices. But it was a reviled Samaritan who showed kindness to the stranger when the Jewish religious leaders passed by the injured man. The illustration turned the tables again on this other lawyer's understanding of the Scriptures. Read the story in Luke 10:25–37.

Sadly, the Middle East today is still a hotbed of bigotry and religious intolerance. Even in that environment, there are remarkable examples of individuals who are demonstrating what it looks like to love their neighbors as Jesus instructed. Tom and JoAnn Doyle are a couple doing just that.

Tom is the executive in charge of Middle Eastern ministry for E3 Partners, a Christian missions organization based in the United

States. He oversees a wide range of ministry and humanitarian efforts throughout that region. Surprisingly, he reports rapid growth in the effectiveness of his work within Muslim countries.

He talks about distributing food and providing medical clinics for Muslim refugees who were living in sprawling makeshift camps in Jordan. E3 is taking care of hundreds of families that fled from the violence in Syria. Thousands more are receiving general assistance. Many of the Muslims are overheard saying things such as, "The Bible people treated us like human beings."

JoAnn has taken teams of Christian women to minister to Muslim women in the Middle East. She said, "God has called us to love them. They are just like we are. They want to be loved. Imagine what they must feel like to be veiled in burkas and invisible to the world.

"Jesus went to the despised and overlooked people. Muslims fit that profile today," added JoAnn. "If you see a veiled woman in a store, look at her and smile. If you can, ask her where she is from. You will be surprised at the warm response that comes back."

What is most exciting to Tom and JoAnn are the large numbers of Muslims who report that Jesus has appeared to them in a dream or vision. Those who have these dreams are drawn to the love they feel coming from *Isa* ("Jesus" in Arabic). These encounters have been happening in dozens of Islamic countries and are so compelling that scores of Muslims are embracing Christ as their Savior. Tom reports that evidence from the field indicates more Muslims have become followers of Jesus in the last decade than in previous centuries combined.

Loving the Neighbor under My Roof?

Seeing what God is doing around the world is inspiring. There is something significant about crossing cultural boundaries to represent the One who called us to love our neighbors.

However, my closest neighbors—my spouse and children—live right under my roof. They should hold the top spot in the second great commandment. But how well have I done with this part of the message?

I remember hearing about how my grandmother kept her family fed during the years following the Great Depression. In the garage she kept a huge burlap sack filled with lima beans that daily found their way onto dinner plates in every kind of concoction she could imagine. Stomachs were full, and the kids of her family, including my dad, accepted these meals as a normal part of life. By today's standards it may seem lacking, yet they had plenty of love to go around.

While my grandmother cared for the family on the home front, my grandfather traveled the western United States by train, selling record albums for a music company. He was often gone for weeks at a time. During those long train rides, he wrote poems and serial stories and mailed them to his wife and children. It was his way of helping bridge the distance and keeping in touch with his family until he returned.

Feeling nostalgic one holiday season, I decided to pull out some home movies from my childhood to show to Kathleen and our children, Brooks and Brianna. The tapes were recorded at Christmastime back in the 1950s when my grandparents and older relatives were still alive. I hoped to give my own family a short history lesson about our heritage.

As the old footage began, the camera slowly scanned the beautiful Christmas tree with its tinsel and lights. Then it unhurriedly swept across the presents at the tree's base. I wondered aloud, "Did we only take pictures of the tree and presents? Where is everybody?" As if on cue, the camera shifted to the semicircle of relatives sitting around the room. This time, the camera moved a bit quicker past my grandparents, parents, sister, aunts, uncles, and cousins only to slow down again after the decorations and gifts came into view. For the camera operator, filming the once-a-year festivities of Christmas was more important than filming family members whom we saw all the time. We were able to see only fleeting images of our cherished relatives, while we were given a good look at 1950s tinsel and presents.

It turned into a convicting object lesson for me about the value of my own family. The moments we enjoy together will not always remain the same. Holiday celebrations are meaningful, but the true gifts are the people sitting around the table, enjoying the experience with us. That inner circle includes our spouses and children.

We shouldn't be surprised that the command to love our neighbors starts first in the home. Caring for our husbands, wives, sons, and daughters is an important first step in accomplishing what Jesus commanded us to do. Even if marriage and children are not in the picture now, we still have many opportunities to successfully live out what Jesus has called us to do.

Definition of Finishing Well

As I thought about how to define what it meant to finish well for the Lord, I chose the two great commandments of Jesus to serve as the foundation. I encourage you to think about what loving God with all your heart, soul, mind, and strength really means, as well as how to practically live out loving your neighbor as yourself. As you do, I would be very interested in reading what *finishing well* means from your perspective. My contact information can be found at the back of this book. Feel free to send your definition or other comments directly to me.

Here is *my* definition for finishing life well:

> *To finish life in right relationship to my God, spouse, family, fellow man, and the work He gave me to do.*

Jesus's two commandments seemed to break naturally into five related areas—God, spouse, family, fellow man, and fulfilling His work. What also factored in for me was being in *right relationship* with each one. This starts first with God, then works its way out from there. Each of the five parts can present its own unique challenges to us. That's why finishing well for the Lord is a lifelong process!

Here is how it could be diagrammed:

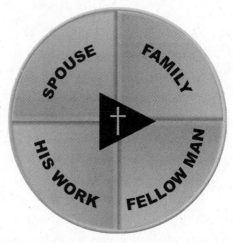

Inner wheel (copyright Bruce Peppin)

God is at the center. A right relationship with Him is crucial to success in the other areas. As I looked at this definition, it seemed rather daunting. Could I truly say I was in right relationship in each area? Honestly, not really. That's where the Almighty being at the heart of life is the key difference. We rely on His strength, not our own, to live this kind of life. Understanding the message of Zechariah 4:6 is an encouragement: "'Not by might nor by power, but by My Spirit,' says the LORD of hosts." God reminds us that human endeavor cannot accomplish His purposes, but He will move mountains for us as we depend on His power.

For me, this definition identified some big areas that I want to work on with God's help. These have eternal value, so I know my efforts are going toward what will last.

As an interesting exercise, try applying the definition to those who have passed away in your family or with others you know. Did anyone finish with all five areas in right relationship? If so, that is inspiring! Getting three or four is commendable, but the real test for us is whether all five are in the picture.

Finish with All Five

I gave a series of presentations during which I shared this definition to over one hundred Christian professionals. I asked them the same question about their families and friends. One might expect this type of audience to score higher marks; however, the answers they gave confirmed my hunch.

Less than 10 percent indicated that the people who had passed on had finished life with all five parts of the definition in right relationship. It appears to be more difficult than we thought.

Is this consistent with what you expected? How did your answers compare?

If you can, find some time in the next few days to write out your own definition of finishing well for the Lord. Or use the one I created. Then place the definition somewhere noticeable to serve as a reminder.

Do you feel God prompting you to work on one particular area of finishing well? Let the following verse be an inspiration: "For I am confident of this very thing, that He who began a good work in you will perfect it until the day of Christ Jesus" (Phil. 1:6).

Moving Mountains Moment

Although Mount Everest is the highest mountain on the earth, it doesn't even make the top-ten list if we consider the other mountains in our solar system. The grand prize goes to Olympus Mons on Mars. It rises sixteen miles high or nearly eighty-five thousand feet! Size doesn't matter to God. He created immense mountains and massive stars by the trillions and scattered them across an endless universe! He created them to incite us to ponder His greatness. When thinking about this, King David wrote, "When I consider Your heavens, the work of Your fingers, the moon and the stars, which You have ordained; what is man that You take thought of him, and the son of man that You care for him? … O LORD, our Lord, how majestic is Your name in all the earth!" (Ps. 8:3–4, 9). I hope you will find this encouraging as you bring your mountains to God for Him to move!

HIGH RISK

Jay and Jan were best friends. Both were talented singers and toured together, inspiring church audiences across the United States. They got married and continued in music ministry until their children were born. The time came to stop traveling and put down roots as staff members at a local congregation. Over the next fifteen years, Jay and Jan brought eight babies into the world and enjoyed the blessings of a large family.

Somewhere around the twenty-year mark in Jay and Jan's marriage, friends were surprised to learn that they were separating. Jay admitted that he wrestled with anger issues from his past, which he'd allowed to spill out onto Jan and the children. Counseling hadn't worked. Jay took what he thought would be a short time away to reduce the tension and try to reconnect with Jan.

He never returned home.

Though he tried to rebuild trust, the wounds were deep between them and the chasm couldn't be bridged. Sadly, financial pressures led to bankruptcy. A year later with hope lost, Jan filed for divorce. She soon remarried, ending the chances of being together with Jay again.

How do best friends get married, have eight children, serve together in ministry, inspire others to follow Jesus, provide marriage counseling, and not be able to hold their own relationship together? The reality is, if it can happen to Jay and Jan, it can happen to any of us.

Gray Divorce

Researchers have coined a phrase to describe what is happening to long-term marriages that break apart. They call it "gray divorce." The *Wall Street Journal* reported in its Life and Culture section that the rate of divorce among Americans aged fifty and older has more than doubled over the last two decades, rising to its highest level on record.[1] Research findings also noted that an increasing percentage of women were seeking the breakup.

We can see the effects of this among our own circle of family and friends. Often, wonderful and caring people experience the impact of divorce, affairs, financial collapse, or other heartbreaking problems. It's very possible that you might be grappling with one of these situations now.

Those of us in midlife are at especially high risk for having something similar happen. I wish it were different, but this is the real world we face.

Every stage of life has its difficulties, but what's been surprising to observe is how concentrated these challenges become as we get older. Rather than seeing an easing of pressures in the later years, many discover a noticeable increase in these stresses. Lest our younger friends think it won't happen to them, unfortunately they're not exempt either.

Hard Realities

Remember all the dreams and goals we had when we started out in life? The future was bright and nothing could stand in our way.

We were like the character of George Bailey in the classic film *It's a Wonderful Life*. He was going to travel the world, build skyscrapers, and leave Bedford Falls far behind. It didn't take long for those dreams to crash around him, to the point where he wished he hadn't been born.

Like George Bailey, the midlife years confront us with many unexpected hard realities:

- Deep regrets
- Crises of faith
- Marriage problems
- Financial difficulties

- Health issues
- Unemployment pressures
- Demands of caring for aging parents
- Struggles with adult children

Dealing with life's hardships is nothing new. Past generations have done that. What's unique for today's midlifers is managing problems that are more severe because of unprecedented societal breakdown and technological change. As a result, those in this life stage are at high risk of buckling under the pressure and derailing.

Any number of poor decisions can result if we're not careful:

- Drifting from God
- Leaving a marriage
- Distancing from family and friends
- Numbing the pain through pornography, alcohol, or drugs
- Pursuing unhealthy relationships leading to affairs and questionable friendships
- Making risky decisions pursuing get-rich-quick schemes and unwise investments

George Bailey recognized the incredible blessings of his life before it was too late. He returned to his family, faced the financial crisis, and "chose to live again." In the closing scene, the entire town arrives at his house to pile up enough money to pay off the debt.

While our problems probably won't be resolved like in a Hollywood movie, *It's a Wonderful Life* reminds us that our family and relationships matter at a deep level. They are a treasure to hold close and guard carefully.

My heart breaks for friends such as Jay and Jan who had a love story that fell apart. There is no need to judge them; they have done enough of that to themselves. What we can do is learn some important lessons from their struggles. One of which is to realize that we are in the midst of a spiritual battle that rages against all we hold dear.

Some surprising statistics surface if we consider how the people in the Bible fared against the difficulties they faced. "There are 2,930 people mentioned in the Bible and we only know significant details for about 100 of them. Of this group only 1/3 appear to have finished well with most failing in the second half of life."[2] If you narrow this list further by selecting only the kings of Israel and Judah after the reign of Solomon, the numbers are even more dismal. There were nineteen kings of Israel; the biblical text records that *all* were evil. There were twenty kings of Judah; the biblical text records that *most* were evil (twelve kings, or 60 percent).

If two-thirds of the people we know from the Bible and most of the kings who reigned did not finish well, then the seriousness of the challenge before us is clear. What is important to remember is that countless people did finish well despite the statistics. It can be done.

Prepare for Normandy

I often stop by Barnes & Noble to browse the latest book releases. During one visit, a title caught my attention that was displayed on a table near the front. It was a large, pictorial volume called *Normandy: Breaching the Atlantic Wall from D-Day to the Breakout and Liberation* by Dominique François.[3] I was immediately drawn into it and found myself transported back in time.

The book chronicled the terrible battle that took place on the beaches of Normandy, France, during the early morning hours of June 6, 1944. Many historians believe this battle, known as D-day, was the turning point of World War II, which eventually led to the defeat of the Nazis.

The pages were filled with wrenching pictures and firsthand accounts of what took place that day. The battle for Omaha Beach was one of the most brutal of the war. The personal heroism displayed by our young soldiers was awe inspiring.

Imagine what it would have been like to be one of those American soldiers that morning. In the night you were moved from large battleships and packed tight with your fellow warriors into amphibious landing crafts that struggled to stay upright in the rough seas. The shallow waters of the beach hid sunken logs topped with explosives ready to blow up your boat. At the landing, you plunged into freezing waves to begin the assault.

The beaches were strewn with thousands of land mines, barbed wire coiled in every direction, and huge multipronged metal "hedgehogs" positioned to defeat tank movement. High above, German machine guns in fortified concrete bunkers shredded the world around you.

Your assignment was to fight your way across that beach and up one-hundred-foot cliffs to take out the enemy in hand-to-hand combat if required. The goal was to control a five-mile stretch of coastline code-named Omaha after the city in Nebraska.

Each soldier with you realized the odds were slim that he would return home alive. Yet he pressed forward to confront a formidable enemy and did not turn back.

We can use the Battle of Normandy as a metaphor of what it's like for many of us to hold our marriages, families, and personal integrity together in today's culture. We're in major combat. Obstacles are everywhere. Casualties surround us. And we are confronted by an Enemy bent on our destruction.

But do we realize it?

If this comparison seems like an overstatement for your situation, then be grateful. Yet I believe Normandy is closer to the environment many of us are facing in our marriages and families.

Battlefield Training

Should our training to protect our loved ones be any less than the training given to those who were sent to defend the freedom of our country? Before ever landing on Omaha Beach, each soldier went through a rigorous boot camp, was trained in battlefield tactics, and was outfitted with the best equipment of that time. He was not only educated about the enemy but also given a grand vision of what he was fighting for. He knew he was a part of something far bigger than his own personal fulfillment and comfort. It was about delivering nations, freeing people, and laying down his life, if necessary, to rescue them.

Walter Ehlers was a twenty-three-year-old staff sergeant on the day he led a squad of soldiers across Normandy's beaches. They fought their way over the sand, scaled the cliffs, and penetrated deep into enemy territory. He single-handedly took out several German machine-gun nests that had pinned down his men, and he killed a roving group of enemy soldiers who were advancing on his position. Even after being severely wounded, he continued to fight to protect those under his charge. His actions on the battlefield were so heroic that he was awarded the Medal of Honor, the United States' highest military commendation.

He spoke at a forum held at the Reagan Presidential Library about his experiences as a soldier on D-day. He emphasized that his faith in God carried him through and gave him courage. He told the crowd of mostly young adults, "Get as much training as possible before you enter the battle. I had two years of combat training before I ever fought on the beaches of Normandy."[4] His advice is a great reminder for us. We must prepare for the battle before us. It will be just as rigorous as Normandy was.

Winston Churchill's Speech

In his first speech as prime minister, Winston Churchill delivered these memorable words to the House of Commons at the beginning of Britain's war with Germany on May 13, 1940:

> I have nothing to offer but blood, toil, tears, and sweat.
> We have before us an ordeal of the most grievous kind. We
> have before us many, many long months of struggle and of

> suffering. You ask, "What is our policy?" I can say: It is to
> wage war, by sea, land, and air, with all our might and with
> all the strength that God can give us; to wage war against a
> monstrous tyranny, never surpassed in the dark, lamentable
> catalogue of human crime. That is our policy. You ask, "What
> is our aim?" I can answer in one word: It is victory.[5]

Churchill stirred England with his sobering words. Yet he also imparted hope that the war could be won. All these years later, our hearts are still moved by the power of what he said and the victory that was achieved.

I wonder how many marriages could be held together if men and women were trained to fight and sacrifice for their relationships with the same intensity that the soldiers demonstrated on the beaches of Normandy some seventy years ago.

Revised Churchill Speech

What might those famous words sound like today if they were adapted to exhort us to hold on to our marriage vows and integrity in the midst of our own Normandy battles? Who would have the boldness to stand up and deliver this type of message on marriage, family, and personal integrity in our churches? It could sound something like this:

> I have nothing to offer but sacrifice, toil, tears, and sweat.
> We have before us an ordeal of the most grievous kind in
> holding our marriages and families together while keeping
> our personal integrity intact. We have before us many, many
> long months and possibly years of struggle and of suffering.
> You ask, "What are we to do?" I can say: It is to wage war by
> every means at our disposal, with all our might and with all
> the strength that God can give us; to wage war against a mon-
> strous Enemy committed to the destruction of our marriages

and everything good in our lives for which many have fallen, forming a dark, lamentable catalog of broken lives. That is our situation. You ask, "What is the outcome?" I can answer in one phrase: It is hearing God say, "Well done, good and faithful servant!"

If I had heard this type of message before I got married, it would have caught my attention. Perhaps I might have worked harder at premarital counseling and been better prepared to handle the challenges that eventually came.

I know this is a sober assessment of the reality we are facing. But can it be anything else given our divorce rates, the brokenness of our families, and the personal failures of God's people? There is no way around dealing with the seriousness of the situation. We must face it head-on and make our stand now.

Winston Churchill and the soldiers fighting on the beaches of Normandy knew what was at stake. They were ready to sacrifice their lives to achieve victory.

While the challenges may seem insurmountable, it is not time to lose heart. We read these inspiring words from God about the spiritual battle we are facing:

> Finally, be strong in the Lord and in the strength of His might. Put on the full armor of God, so that you will be able to stand firm against the schemes of the devil. For our struggle is not against flesh and blood, but against the rulers, against the powers, against the world forces of this darkness, against the spiritual forces of wickedness in the heavenly places. Therefore, take up the full armor of God, so that you will be able to resist in the evil day, and having done everything, to stand firm. (Eph. 6:10–13)

Let's hold on to this promise from the Lord and determine to engage the battle on behalf of our spouses, children, and personal integrity even if it means scaling cliffs to succeed. It definitely will be worth the cost.

Moving Mountains Moment

Instead of Mount McKinley or Mount Kilimanjaro, the mountains of midlife could be named Mount Regrets, Mount Faith, Mount Marriage, Mount Health, and Mount Finance, among others. Each presents looming problems that are difficult to manage. They can seem like an entire mountain range of dilemmas to deal with. The apostle Peter told us to cast "all your anxiety on Him, because He cares for you" (1 Pet. 5:7). God knows every detail of our lives and is with us to help us move these mountains as we depend on Him for strength and guidance.

PART TWO

THE CORE

Understanding the Five Priorities for Moving Mountains

4

GOING DEEPER

My life fell apart in May 2000. It came as quite a blow as I prided myself in my ability to manage problems and press through obstacles. There was a depth to the brokenness in my marriage and family that left me at a loss. God was nowhere to be found. He was distant from my daily experience. Yet here I was working for a Christian organization. I thought of resigning.

Normally, I could "perform" my way out of a conflict. By that, I mean I could exert an all-out effort to settle the crisis *externally*, powering my way through to "peace at all costs" even if it meant sidestepping what was happening on a heart level. My intention was to deal with those deeper issues later and do the hard work of getting to the core of what was wrong. Unfortunately, not much was ever resolved. As a result, my relational efforts slumped into hollow actions of duty and obligation.

In marriage, no wife (or husband) wants to be related to out of duty. That also holds true in our relationship with God. Dutifully going through the motions can last only so long.

When matters of faith are talked about, we can place ourselves somewhere along a spiritual continuum. One end represents a deep commitment to God, an active follower of Jesus Christ. On the other is unbelief or disappointment in God. If I had to mark my spot on the line during this time, it would have tilted far in this latter direction.

Unbelief or disappointment in God ————×————— Deep commitment to God

While I had been a follower of Jesus for many years, I was in a huge crisis of faith. The expectations I had for God and what He should be doing in my life and family had been dashed. Here are some notes I wrote in my journal during that time:

> "I feel depressed, despairing, distant, and disconnected from God."

> "I am afraid that nothing will change if I reach my hand toward heaven."

> "I am bound up under this load and will probably retreat to my safe harbor of duty, obligation, and resignation again."

If you identify with anything I have described, I know the burden and disappointment you are feeling. I had lost connection not only with my wife but also with God. I was stuck and couldn't see a way out. The negative circumstances of my life continued to escalate, soon forcing me to realize the image I'd created of having everything under control was fake.

Thirty Days Off in Crisis

Not long after this I was standing outside my boss's office. Taking a deep breath, I knocked on his door and walked in. I stumbled a little trying to find the words to explain what was going on and that I needed to take a month off. He listened and then nodded in agreement. He asked if it was okay to pull in his leadership team, my colleagues, to pray for me. Previously, I would have balked at being so vulnerable before them. Now, with the "have it all together" image crumpled around my ankles, I was ready for their support. It was humbling, but my journey out of the darkness had begun.

I needed some counseling and got the name of a psychiatrist. He agreed to talk with me but indicated we would need several days of sessions. Arrangements were made to meet at a retreat center near Glenwood Springs in the Colorado Rocky Mountains.

The first session was intense. With a few probing questions, the emotional floodgates opened, compelling me to make a brutally honest assessment of my life. I shared transparently, which I had seldom done before. With more skillful questions, the layers of my heart were exposed.

After I had been in a couple of sessions, he started to confront my choices and the way I had been living. Some of his more memorable statements had set me back, but they had also rung true: "You can't go on being clinically depressed" and "You can't continue living a lobotomized life." I knew I was in a lousy emotional state, but this confirmed the worst.

What he said next stunned me. He essentially said I was living as a practical agnostic. I was acting as though God didn't even exist. If I stayed on this track without changing course, he wasn't sure I would hold on to my faith, much less my marriage! Later I recognized that God had used the interaction of our sessions to force open my heart.

God's Terms, Not Mine

I discovered at the core of my life was a belief that *God had to operate according to my terms and conditions.* Didn't I know what would make me happy and how life was supposed to turn out? However, there was a problem with this approach. God wasn't cooperating or doing what I demanded. I felt thwarted at each step.

The turning point for me was finally figuring out that I had it all backward. I needed to live according to God's terms, not my own. I had to surrender to His plans and drop my unrealistic expectations about how life should be. While it might appear to be an obvious conclusion, the awareness of God's connection to my daily activities was not clear to me.

One of the most notorious kings in the Bible had to learn this lesson too. He was a Babylonian despot named Nebuchadnezzar, who possessed an unbridled ego. He conquered the known world and lifted himself up to godlike status. We meet him in the book of Daniel.

Nebuchadnezzar had an alarming dream one night soon after he had created a ninety-foot-tall gold statue (possibly of himself) that people were commanded to worship. Persian magicians and sorcerers were called in to his bedchamber to interpret the dream, but none could do so. Daniel was brought in and delivered the following message from God:

> This is the decree of the Most High, which has come upon my lord the king: that you be driven away from mankind and your dwelling place be with the beasts of the field, and you be given grass to eat like cattle and be drenched with the dew of heaven; and seven periods of time will pass over you, until you recognize that the Most High is ruler over the realm of mankind and bestows it on whomever He wishes. And ... after you recognize that it is Heaven that rules." (Dan. 4:24–26)

The last phrase, "and after you recognize that it is Heaven that rules," expresses this idea that we live according to God's terms and not our own. There are divine rules in this universe that have been put in place by the Lord for our benefit. We don't make them; He does.

Nebuchadnezzar learned the hard way by being sentenced to live like a beast in the field for seven years, eating grass and going crazy. After Nebuchadnezzar completed those years, God had his attention and he was a changed man. Here is what he said after regaining his sanity:

> But at the end of that period, I, Nebuchadnezzar, raised my eyes toward heaven and my reason returned to me, and I blessed the Most High and praised and honored Him who lives forever.... I, Nebuchadnezzar, praise, exalt and honor the King of heaven, for all His works are true and His ways just, and He is able to humble those who walk in pride. (Dan. 4:34, 37)

God isn't going to conform to our demands, because He is working at an infinitely higher level. Apart from His direction, our big plans often keep us circling around in a cul-de-sac. John Eldredge described the process God uses to break us away from living self-centeredly to living fully for Him:

> God must, from time to time, and sometimes very insistently, disrupt our lives *so that* we release our grasping of life here and now. Usually through pain. God is asking us to let go of the things we love and have given our hearts to, so that we can give our hearts even more fully to him. He thwarts us in our attempts to make life work, so that our efforts fail, and we must face the fact that we don't really look to God for life. Our first reaction is usually to get angry with him, which only serves to make the point. Don't you hear people say, "Why did God let this happen?" far more than you hear them say, "Why aren't I more fully given over to God?"[1]

The days following my counseling retreat were spent renewing my heart and relationships. I took a trip with Kathleen for some needed days away with her and climbed my first "fourteener" mountain in Colorado called Uncompahgre Peak (described p. 36). Spending time in the alpine wilderness was also a great place to meet with God.

I continued my journey out of despair and defeat. At least I was now heading in the right direction and wasn't wandering aimlessly in the woods.

God's Heart toward Us

At this point, you may be feeling as I did—that God is distant and disconnected from your life. Or you are disappointed in Him for the hurt and wounds you have received over the years. Maybe He hasn't seemed to be a good heavenly Father, given your past experiences.

It might be surprising to realize how God views His relationship with us. In Isaiah 65:1–2, He said, "I was ready to respond, but no one asked for help. I was ready to be found, but no one was looking for me. I said,

'Here I am, here I am!' to a nation that did not call on my name. All day long I opened my arms to a rebellious people" (NLT).

God is actively reaching out to us all the time, but with little success. It pinpoints the problem that we want a relationship with God only on our terms, not on His terms. That's a sure path to disillusionment.

God relates to us in the most personal way. Read what He says regarding His heart for you and me from Isaiah 43:1–4:

- I created you.
- Do not be afraid.
- I have ransomed you.
- I have called you by name.
- You are Mine.
- I will be with you when you go through deep waters or walk through fire.
- I am the Lord your God.
- I am the Holy One of Israel.
- I am your Savior.
- You are precious in My sight.
- You are honored.
- I love you.

That's quite a list from just a few verses. It says a lot about God's genuine care for us. What do we do with that? Hopefully, we respond by opening up our lives to Him. A good place to start would be evaluating whether we have set up terms for our lives that God must work within. Do we act as though these requirements indicate if God loves us? If He doesn't live up to them, will we keep Him at a distance or choose not to believe at all? Writing down your terms can be helpful. You may be surprised at how long the list is, and it might explain why you are disappointed with God.

The daring step for us is what we will do with our lists. Opening our hearts to the King of heaven is risky, and it makes us vulnerable to disappointment if things don't go our way. But God is trustworthy! Toss your list out the window. In its place, write a new list filled with God's promises. On it, add lines such as "Follow Me," "Trust in Me," "I will show up for you," and "Remember, I love you." It might be light on specifics for your situation, but you can rest assured that it will be full of purpose, hope, and power.

F. W. Pitt, a British pastor (1859–1943), wrote a poem called "Maker of the Universe," which articulates a depth to God's love that people rarely consider. Keeping a long list of requirements for God to perform loses its appeal when compared to the vast love He has demonstrated for us. Here is how it reads:

> The Maker of the universe,
> As Man, for man was made a curse.
> The claims of Law which He had made,
> Unto the uttermost He paid.
> His holy fingers made the bough,
> Which grew the thorns that crowned His brow.
> The nails that pierced His hand were mined,
> In secret places He designed.
> He made the forest whence there sprung,
> The tree on which His body hung.
> He died upon a cross of wood,
> Yet made the hill on which it stood.
> The sky that darkened o'er His head,
> By Him above the earth was spread.
> The sun that hid from Him its face,
> By His decree was poised in space.
> The spear which spilled His precious blood,

Was tempered in the fires of God.
The grave in which His form was laid,
Was hewn in rocks His hands had made.
The throne on which He now appears,
Was His from everlasting years.
But a new glory crowns His brow,
And every knee to Him shall bow!
The Maker of the universe.

My heart was profoundly touched when I first read this poem. Not only did Jesus willingly bear the sins of mankind on the cross, but He also created the very implements used in His torture and death (Col. 1:16). While difficult to comprehend, this truth further expresses the magnitude of God's love for us.

Even with this added understanding about the Lord, our lives can still feel trapped under the weight of overbearing circumstances. It's so easy to question if God is there, but it is often during our times of doubt that He shows up in unexpected ways.

Luke 13 tells the extraordinary story of a woman who encountered Jesus in the midst of intense, long-term suffering.

The drama unfolds in verse 11, describing a pitiful woman who shuffled, bent double, into the synagogue. Her anguish, caused by an evil spirit, had lasted for nearly two decades. Living each day would have been utter misery.

With head down, seeing nothing but the floor, she feebly made her way inside. It's worth noting she still came to worship God. In some desperate way, her faith in the Lord held firm. Little did she know that her world was going to change completely moments later.

She was unaware that Jesus was present, but He saw her. The voice that spoke the universe into existence gently called her to come over. Fear and uncertainty may have gripped her, yet she dared to draw near.

Jesus laid His hands on her and spoke the command, "Woman, you are freed from your sickness." Immediately she stood up straight and began glorifying God (Luke 13:12–13). Her years of trusting faithfully saw their fulfillment in an instant.

This encounter illustrates a pattern we experience. We're all stuck and "bent double" at some point in life. Jesus sees us. He knows our condition, and He calls us to come over. We have a choice to make. Will we dare to surrender ourselves to Him? He can bring healing and freedom to our lives.

If we're in the midst of an "unbendable" situation, let's keep a firm grip on our faith, knowing that Jesus sees us. His intervention will come.

Author Ann Voskamp described the situation this way: "If we are dying of thirst, passively reading books about water quenches little; the only way to quench the parched mouth is to close the book and dip the hand into water and bring it to the lips. If we thirst, we'll have to drink."[2]

Just like scooping a hand into the water to quench our thirst, we must take a step of faith to pursue a personal relationship with the God of heaven. He has already made the first move toward us. Now it is our turn to respond to His invitation.

Our Heart toward God

I sat in the audience listening to a message that gripped my heart. The man speaking had been on the top-ten list of ultramarathoners for his age of forty-seven. He was also the successful pastor of a thousand-member church when a drastic turn of events occurred.

John Stumbo said it began with flu-like symptoms nearly two years earlier. *Nothing to worry about*, he thought. He then described what started happening in rapid succession to his body: "Soon, sores stormed my mouth. It seemed that whatever was attacking my body began flaring up everywhere. My inner cheeks, gums, and tongue looked like a miniature minefield. Next, my digestive and urinary system started to go haywire. Loss of appetite, agonizing constipation and a growing concern about my kidneys took my 'bleh' to new depths. Meanwhile, blood tests revealed that my muscle enzymes were going crazy, registering many times higher than that of a normal person."

His weight soared from 190 pounds to 270 pounds and then plummeted to 140 pounds. He went from the picture of health to near physical collapse in a matter of weeks. He had to step down from the church and started running a new kind of race—a marathon through emotional and spiritual darkness.

But the worst was yet to come. His body was in such turmoil that he lost his ability to swallow. "I couldn't swallow anything. I had to spit saliva onto a spit rag that was carried everywhere. I learned that swallowing was a very complex function. Soon after that I had to have a feeding tube installed in my stomach. Every day for eighteen months, seven cans of nutrients were poured down that tube to keep me alive. Praise God for a wife who kept her vows and believed in me."

His faith in God was rocked to the core. "When you're trashed inside, it's okay to hold on to someone else's faith when you have none. One of the names of God is the 'Lion of Judah.' I quickly realized that He is not a tame lion and wouldn't jump through the hoops I wanted Him to jump through."

On a summer vacation driving out to see family in Tennessee, they stopped to get some ice cream, which John liked to swish in his mouth before having to spit it out. After driving again on the highway, the ice cream unexpectedly slipped down his throat. He sat back shocked, questioning what had just occurred. Then he said that a "quiet, silent miracle took place on that road. I carefully tasted the ice cream again to see what happened. Again, it went down my throat. I motioned for Joanna and the kids to watch. The ice cream disappeared like before. I was able to swallow!"

The progress was very slow, but it was the beginning of a recovery. There were levels of peace and joy during those eighteen months of ordeal that he could hardly believe. He came to the realization that "you could live a fulfilled life without all the answers or no answers."

It was inspiring to hear him say, "God was greater than the disease that attacked me. God was in it with me and He is good. We're in this life for Him. It's His story. Keep writing yours with that in mind."[3]

John was able to scoop his hand in the water and find that God quenched his thirst in the midst of extreme suffering. He concluded that God was good even if it meant the loss of swallowing for the rest of his life. At some time in our lives, we will need to answer the same questions: Is God with us? Is He good? John would encourage us to answer each of those questions with a firm yes!

The Choice before Us

In *The Last Battle*, C. S. Lewis's final book in the Chronicles of Narnia series, some dwarfs are sitting huddled together. They are clinging to one another for protection, believing a battle is still raging around them. They don't realize that the great lion, Aslan, has come and rescued Narnia. The ropes around their hands and feet have been removed, and the fighting is over. Tash, a multiarmed, vulture-like monster, has been defeated. Surrounding the dwarfs now is a deep blue sky, groves of trees filled with beautiful fruit, and friends waiting to welcome them to Aslan's world. But they refuse to believe it, preferring to remain hunkered down in the comfortable darkness of their old existence.

Aslan attempts to reach them:

> He came close to the Dwarfs and gave a low growl: low, but
> it set all the air shaking. But the Dwarfs said to one another,
> "Hear that? That's the gang at the other end of the stable.
> Trying to frighten us. They do it with a machine of some

kind. Don't take any notice. They won't take *us* in again!" …
"You see," said Aslan. "They will not let us help them. They
have chosen cunning instead of belief. Their prison is only in
their own minds, yet they are in that prison; and so afraid of
being taken in that they cannot be taken out."[4]

How can we miss the outstretched arms of an amazing God who
pursues us day after day? Like the dwarfs who could not see Aslan standing in front of them, Scripture says we also have a veil over our eyes: "The
god of this world has blinded the minds of the unbelieving so that they
might not see the light of the gospel of the glory of Christ, who is the
image of God" (2 Cor. 4:4). Two factors appear to be in play: our own
unbelief and the Enemy of our souls who takes advantage of our unbelief.

One of the greatest examples of spiritual blindness is what the apostle
John recorded about the people who saw Jesus during His time on earth.
He was deity incarnate standing before them, yet sadly John wrote: "He
was in the world, and the world was made through Him, and the world
did not know Him. He came to His own, and those who were His own
did not receive Him" (John 1:10–11). This is convicting because I have
often acted the same way and missed what the Lord was doing in front of
me. Our unbelief can be so overpowering.

Not long ago I heard my colleague Paul McCusker present a talk
about what he thought was going on in the spiritual realm with the
Enemy of our souls. While shocking, it is a frightening possibility. Here
is a portion of what he said:

> Apart from God we are simply members of the demon's food
> chain. We are like cattle. We are their food or waste! Demons
> want us to be as much at home on earth as possible. They
> encourage our lethargy, comfort, routine, dullness or thrills—
> anything to make us forget about heaven and God's country.

There is a reason Satan is called the devourer for that is what he does. He wants us to believe we're kings and sovereigns on earth to fatten us up so we can be eaten later! He would have us give up when we get close to the finish line and drag us down to defeat. We belong to God and His realm, but often forget where our true home is. The question to ask ourselves is "Am I doing the bidding of my master—God, or am I only a part of the demonic food chain?"

The group was appalled after hearing Paul's graphic description of the demonic world. The brutish idea of being fattened up as prey seemed incomprehensible. His comments gave new meaning to the verse "Be of sober spirit, be on the alert. Your adversary, the devil, prowls around like a roaring lion, seeking someone to devour" (1 Pet. 5:8). Peter used a strong word for "devour," meaning to "drink down, swallow up, and destroy." This referenced the words of Jesus when He described Satan who "comes only to steal and kill and destroy" (John 10:10). When put in these words, those outside of faith in Christ are in dire trouble.

The Bible is clear in presenting the reality of these spiritual forces of wickedness. Fortunately, those who have submitted themselves to Jesus are not at the mercy of these foes. We gladly read, "For He rescued us from the domain of darkness, and transferred us to the kingdom of His beloved Son" (Col. 1:13).

For some of us, the issue of salvation in Jesus Christ has still not been settled in our hearts. We haven't surrendered our lives to follow Him. The apostle Peter stressed the importance of this point when he said, "And there is salvation in no one else; for there is no other name under heaven that has been given among men by which we must be saved" (Acts 4:12).

In his book *Nearing Home*, Billy Graham talked about the common struggle many have to believe that something more awaits them beyond this present life.

But how do we know this life isn't the end? How do we know Heaven isn't just wishful thinking on our part? God has revealed Heaven's reality to us in various ways. For example, within each of us is an inner sense or feeling that death is not the end, that there must be something beyond the grave. Even if we deny it or ignore it, this inner yearning is still there—and it is universal. Where did it come from? The Bible says God placed it within us: He "set eternity in the hearts of men" (Ecclesiastes 3:11).[5]

What an appealing phrase—eternity in our hearts—to describe our inner longings for something more than what this earth offers. Fortunately, there are ways to satisfy the yearnings we feel.

Going Deeper with God

God wants us to pursue Him and leave aside our paltry expectations of what life should be like. He delights in revealing His grand plans and purposes; but such revelations flow out of a growing relationship with Him, not a brief encounter. While there are no shortcuts to intimacy with the glorious Trinity—Father, Son, and Holy Spirit—we have a standing invitation to draw near to Him (Heb. 4:16). By responding to this offer from heaven, our lives can avoid being lumped in with those whom C. S. Lewis poignantly described as being "half-hearted creatures, fooling about with drink and sex and ambition when infinite joy is offered us, like an ignorant child who wants to go on making mud pies in a slum because he cannot imagine what is meant by the offer of a holiday at the sea."[6]

Let's accept that offer of a holiday at the sea! The adventure of going deeper in our relationship with God is of priceless value.

Read these closing words aloud as if they were written by Jesus, who is personally inviting you into a closer relationship with Him:

Dear (your name),

I invite you to really know Me, to worship Me, to understand who I am. When you do, everything will change! Study My ways and take in My glory. I am calling you to Myself.

Remember, I fed the five thousand. I walked on the water. I conquered death. I am love. I am all the things your heart desires. Come to Me! Do not be afraid. The narrow path in following Me is never the easy way, but it is where life, fulfillment, and the hope of heaven are found.

Place your trust completely in Me. Receive the salvation offered to you through My death and resurrection. I paid the price for your sin so you wouldn't have to.

Believe in My promises. Trust in My power. Live in My love. Step forth to fulfill all that I will put on your heart to accomplish. Someday you will wonder why you spent so much time worrying about your problems.

You will be a channel through which My Spirit will flow. Your life will be a blessing to many people. Be confident in all that I will do through you.

Join Me and let's begin our journey together today.

Moving Mountains Moment

When we ask God to move the mountains that obstruct our lives, we usually have an expectation regarding how the details should be resolved and the timing for their resolution. These expectations can set us up for disappointment if we try to make the Almighty conform to our limited understanding of the situation. It doesn't work that way. He is the One who knows exactly what needs to happen, and our job is to drop our conditions and follow Him in faith, trusting Him to deliver the answer. These verses remind us how uniquely God can work to remove the mountains in our lives: "Do not call to mind the former things, or ponder things of the past. Behold, I will do something new, now it will spring forth; will you not be aware of it? I will even make a roadway in the wilderness, rivers in the desert" (Isa. 43:18–19).

5

MR. AND MRS.

In 1963, Capitol Records released the song "I Want to Hold Your Hand" by a new British band called the Beatles. The song was an instant success, moving to the number one spot on the Billboard Hot 100 chart. There was an innocence to the music and lyrics that was disarming. A few years later in 1966, the band's lyrics progressed dramatically to "I'll make love to you if you want me to" ("Love You To" from *Revolver*). The culture quickly followed suit, resetting the expectations for how a man and a woman should relate. Unfortunately, married love wasn't in mind.

Billboard's top love song of all time is "Endless Love" by Diana Ross and Lionel Richie. They sang, "Two hearts that beat as one, our lives have just begun ... forever I'll hold you close in my arms." Who wouldn't want to experience a love like that? But were they singing about two married lovers?

I must admit to being a bit jaded. When I see a couple holding hands, cuddling, and smiling as they interact, I think, *They probably aren't married*. And most of the time I'm right. The wedding rings are missing. The scene contrasts starkly to a married couple I watched recently at a restaurant who stopped looking at their smartphones only long enough to order from the menu. There was little conversation except when they selected the food, received the meal, and paid the bill. Why is that? What happens to us after we say, "I do," to the person we love most in the world? For many husbands and wives, the promise of endless love succumbs to endless disappointment.

Given the high expectations placed on our marriages, how we connect with our spouses can be one of the most challenging mountains to be moved. Long-term success is definitely possible, but it will require far more courage, humility, and forgiveness than we ever imagined when we first got married.

Many have already experienced the heartache of divorce. It can happen to the best of us. But divorce does not disqualify us from living a life that finishes well for the Lord.

It is important to remember that God continues to work in our life regardless of what has happened in the past. His love toward us is not diminished in any way. God is in the business of redeeming poor choices. Brennan Manning knew this to be true. He was divorced, a former Franciscan priest, and a recovering alcoholic. Yet his experience of God's love was so deep that he devoted his life to helping people grasp the depth of God's love for them. In his book *The Furious Longing of God*, he wrote:

> The God I've come to know by sheer grace, the Jesus I met in the grounds of my own self, has furiously loved me regardless of my state—grace or disgrace. And why? For His love is never, never, never based on our performance, never conditioned by our moods—of elation or depression. The furious love of God knows no shadow of alteration or change. It is reliable. And always tender.[1]

The apostle Paul wrote beautifully about God's profound love toward us. Let's keep this in mind as we plunge into the discussion about renewing our relationship as husband and wife.

> For I am convinced that neither death, nor life, nor angels, nor principalities, nor things present, nor things to come, nor powers, nor height, nor depth, nor any other created thing, will be able to separate us from the love of God, which is in Christ Jesus our Lord. (Rom. 8:38–39)

An Honest Assessment

First, let me state the obvious. It is risky to be transparent with others about our marital problems. We're afraid to be vulnerable and to admit we need help. It's safer to hide behind a thin veneer of respectability. That's why we're surprised when we learn a friend is getting a divorce—there was no outward indication that anything was wrong!

The irony is, had the couple been daring enough to share their plight, they would have found support among many friends who could have identified with them. Instead of being alone, they were members with everyone else of a large association called *the community of the broken.*

I saw something similar to this scenario play out in front of me a few years ago. A business colleague I had known for over two decades was calling it quits after thirty years of marriage. He was a gifted Christian leader whose ministry skills strengthened religious organizations across the world.

Through our correspondence, I discovered he had struggled with difficulties in his marriage for a long time. He had kept them hidden, not knowing what to do because of his leadership role. As the years rolled by, the situation reached the breaking point.

Because my wife and I had gone through marital counseling on several occasions, I was familiar with the rocky terrain they were maneuvering. I invited him to stay on the path with me and to compare notes on the marriage journey. I tried to assure him the relationship with his wife was worth holding on to even if it seemed hopeless. I also shared about the weightiness of the vow we had made to each other as husbands and wives.

A commitment intended to last a lifetime is not a light matter. If we're honest, sometimes a wedding ring can feel like it weighs one hundred pounds. My friend identified with that, but he was weary and couldn't see a way forward.

Our communication ran its course and eventually stopped. I heard later that his marriage ended because of another woman. I was not angry, and I grieved for him and his wife, wondering what might have been. Few relationships can survive the intrusion of another paramour who competes for our heart, especially when we're vulnerable. To expand our peripheral vision on this, let us look at what the marriage vow means to God.

God's View of the Marriage Vow

Not surprisingly, God has a lot to say on this subject. The Bible begins with a marriage (Adam and Eve, Gen. 1:26–31) and ends with a marriage (the marriage supper of the Lamb, Rev. 19:9). In many places, God described Himself as a husband to Israel and she as His wife. Furthermore, the creation of marriage and family on earth (husband-wife-child) reveals a glimpse into the nature of the Trinity in heaven (Father-Holy Spirit-Son).

Buried in Ezekiel 16 is one of the most striking passages in the Bible that expresses God's heart toward marriage. He described His marital vow to Israel and what it was like to be married to His earthly bride. Every husband and wife would benefit from studying this passage to learn more deeply what it means to love each other in a committed marriage relationship. It will definitely challenge you.

The chapter opens with God speaking to Jerusalem (representing Israel) and recounts for her the story of their courtship. God explained her beginning as a baby abandoned in the field and left to die (which often happened to newborn girls at the time). She came from parents who cast her away without love.

God rescued her from death and provided protection as she grew up. Later, when she came of age, He chose her to be His bride.

As we might expect, the marriage God had with Israel was deeply troubled from the beginning. She was a spouse who quickly took His kindness for granted, was neglectful, was selfish, broke her vow, committed adultery, and walked away from their relationship. The lengths God went to in seeking to restore His marriage with her were amazing.

God as Husband and Israel as Wife

Here are some observations from Ezekiel 16 that provide insight into the type of husband God was toward His wife, Israel, and how she behaved to Him. The love described here was lavish with nothing being held back.

God as a husband:

> I nurtured you when others rejected you (vv. 3–5).
>
> I met your needs when you were hurting (vv. 6–7).
>
> I loved you dearly, married you, and called you Mine (v. 8).
>
> I blessed you in every way possible (vv. 9–14).
>
> I gave Myself fully to you (v. 14).

Take a close look at these verses again. How does the love we express to our spouses compare? If we had to measure ourselves against this example, how would we size up? I'm wincing as I think about it!

In return for the intimate love showered on her, one would expect Israel to draw near to her husband. Let's see how she responded to His kindness.

Israel as a wife:

> I am beautiful and popular (v. 15).
>
> I feel trapped as a wife and desire other relationships (v. 15).
>
> I can do what I want with my life and possessions (vv. 16–19).
>
> I will lead my children however I think best even if it's wrong (vv. 20–21).
>
> I reject You and will make my own decisions (vv. 22–29).

Rather than embrace her husband's love, Israel was consumed with self-centered choices. She failed to see all the blessings that resulted from her marriage. Rather than staying home and loving her spouse, she looked outside for others to meet her needs.

What does this say about the tendency of the human heart? How can we be surrounded by lavish love and yet miss or, even worse, reject it? Is it possible that we could be overlooking some of those blessings right now in our marriages?

The chapter goes on to describe the horrific downward spiral brought on by the choices of one marriage partner. Verse 25 is one of the most graphic in all Scripture, describing how God's wife eventually prostituted herself with anyone who came by. It seemed to be a hopeless situation.

For 99.9 percent of us, this marriage would be over. There's no way we would remain with an adulterous spouse who treated us that way, right?

God's Heart for His Bride

Yet God's incredible love is on display for our benefit in the final four verses of the chapter. He is taking us deep into His heart to consider a level of forgiveness beyond what we might think possible. Here is what He said to His wife after all she had done to Him:

> I will honor My marriage vow even though you have broken yours (v. 60).
>
> I will reestablish My marriage with you and begin our relationship again (v. 62).
>
> I have forgiven you for all that you have done to Me (v. 63).

Let the implications of these verses sink in for a moment. This response from God was so profound that His wife was shocked back to her senses. She remembered what she had done and was ashamed of it (vv. 61, 63).

I don't believe this text is saying we must always stay with an adulterous spouse or remain in an abusive relationship. Rather, could it be an attempt by God to radically alter our thinking about the brokenness and dysfunction we find in our spouses and marital relationships?

Could it be possible that we have more room in our hearts to extend forgiveness than we previously thought? On a human level we don't possess this type of love. It comes only through a deep relationship with the Lord, whose Spirit fills our hearts with divine love.

Romans 5:5 describes it this way: "Hope does not disappoint, because the love of God has been poured out within our hearts through the Holy Spirit who was given to us."

Marriage Questions to Ponder

This section of Ezekiel 16 certainly stretches our understanding of the marriage vow and God's heart for His bride. How far would we be willing to go to honor the vows we made to our spouses and ultimately to the Lord? Let's personalize it even further by asking the following questions:

> What if one of God's purposes in my life is to glorify Him in
> a troubled marriage as a testimony to a hurting world?
> What does God want from me in a broken and exhausted
> marital relationship?
> If I knew that in five years God would show up in a miraculous
> way in my marriage, would I hold on and remain faithful?

Tough questions for sure! How would you answer them? What if God is up to something far greater in our lives than we imagine?

Our Lives as Living Parables for God?

We can't stop now in asking God to reveal more of His heart regarding marriage. But get ready; He is going to turn the tables on us.

In Ezekiel 16, God was the central figure in the story illustrating an astounding love for His wife. Through reading these compelling verses, I am convicted about the puniness of my love for my wife.

Next, God looked to demonstrate His love on a human level. The man selected for this intimidating assignment was named Hosea. His prophetic ministry (mid-750s BC) to the northern kingdom of Israel lasted more than fifty years, spanning the reigns of its last seven kings.

His life exemplified strict obedience to the Lord and boldness to speak divine truth to the apostate nation.

Then God asked him to do the unthinkable—go marry a prostitute! Hosea must have been dumbfounded. "You want me to do what?" A prophet of the Almighty taking that extreme cultural misstep was inconceivable.

The book bearing Hosea's name in the Old Testament explains what happened. At the start of Hosea's prophetic ministry, God told His prophet,

> "Go, take to yourself a wife of harlotry and have children of
> harlotry; for the land commits flagrant harlotry, forsaking the
> LORD." So he went and took Gomer the daughter of Diblaim,
> and she conceived and bore him a son. (Hosea 1:2–3)

You couldn't find two people more incompatible than Hosea and Gomer, a prophet of God and a prostitute. How awkward it must have been as they started living together with nothing in common. Love was not in the picture (yet). Hosea was only doing what he was told, but his heart was not in it. Gomer merely saw the marriage proposal as a way to get food and shelter. Her heart wasn't in it either. Both were unaware they had been chosen to reveal God's love to an estranged nation.

Gomer didn't warm up to the idea of having a husband or children. Her life paralleled Israel's attitude as a wife toward God. The second chapter of Hosea reveals how bad the situation was. In her heart, she was still a prostitute. She didn't care that her actions were shameful or that she continually sought to return to her former life. "For their mother has played the harlot; she who conceived them has acted shamefully. For she said, 'I will go after my lovers, who give me my bread and my water, my wool and my flax, my oil and my drink'" (Hosea 2:5).

God lamented that Israel, like Gomer, did not perceive the goodness of her husband. She was oblivious to all the kindness that was coming to her: "For she does not know that it was I who gave her the grain, the new wine and oil, and lavished on her silver and gold" (v. 8).

Sometime during the early years of her marriage with the demands of raising three children, Gomer reached a breaking point. We don't know the reasons, but she was done with being a wife and mother. She left the family and returned to her life as a prostitute. The text does not say how long she was away or that Hosea was in a hurry to bring her back.

Gomer's self-serving plans fell apart right away. She became enslaved to a man who may have been her pimp or a creditor. Her visions of freedom were shattered. Perhaps as she spent lonely days in a hovel being mistreated as a prostitute, her thoughts wandered back to the life she had spent with Hosea and her children.

In it all, God was working on Hosea's heart. The prophet had forgotten why God told him to marry Gomer—his marriage to Gomer was a living parable of God's great love toward Israel. The day finally came when God told Hosea, "Go get Gomer!" Hosea wrote about it:

> Then the LORD said to me, "Go again, love a woman who is loved by her husband, yet an adulteress, even as the LORD loves the sons of Israel, though they turn to other gods and love raisin cakes." So I bought her for myself for fifteen shekels of silver and a homer and a half of barley. Then I said to her, "You shall stay with me for many days. You shall not play the harlot, nor shall you have a man; so I will also be toward you." (Hosea 3:1–3)

The Message Bible states it more directly: "Then GOD ordered me, 'Start all over: Love your wife again … your cheating wife. Love her the way I, GOD, love the Israelite people'" (v. 1).

Even though Gomer was bought for less than the price of a slave (see Exod. 21:32), she possessed great value to God and to her husband.

Hosea and Gomer spoke at length in the days following her release. He told her, "You are my wife, and we are going to live together for a long time. Your past life is over. We are going to have a relationship with each other that excludes everyone else."

I believe Gomer finally realized, after being purchased from slavery, that Hosea was a caring man who was willing to go to any lengths possible to redeem her from her poor choices. There is no reason to doubt she remained with Hosea from that point forward. It is highly probable she grew to love him and her children. For his part, Hosea forgave Gomer and loved her as his wife. It was a remarkable turnaround. Hosea's fifty-year ministry was deeply influenced by his marriage to Gomer, who taught him that God's love was unconditional, forgiving, and long-suffering.

Here are two important questions that come out of Hosea's story:

1. How far are you willing to go to love your spouse? As far as Hosea?
2. Is God asking you to be a living parable of His love to your spouse and to a hurting world?

Hosea and Gomer overcame giant obstacles to their marriage. Consider the following as God's letter of invitation to you regarding the barriers your marriage is facing:

Dear (your name),

I am calling to you, as I did Hosea, to love your wife (or husband) sacrificially and with kindness. This is the way I love My wife, Israel. As you do this, I will meet you in every moment, filling you with grace and forgiveness. Your life will be a living parable of My love for the world. My desire for an intimate relationship with Israel continues even in the face of her rejection, neglect, or wrongdoing, which I hope is the case with you toward your wife (or husband). I know this is not easy. Rely on My strength to empower you! Find ways to connect to her (or his) broken and wounded heart. Pursue Me most of all! You are just beginning to know more about My extravagant love. As you move forward to love your wife (or husband) as I love Israel, a whole new relationship with Me will open up. And the healing of hearts can take place. Are you ready? Good! Let's get started!

Acceptance and Faithfulness

As we are on the journey to more capably love our spouse, we can benefit from looking at couples who have gotten it right over decades of marriage. One couple who models the qualities needed is Tony and Becky Metcalf. They've been married thirty-eight years. As I talked with them, I was intrigued to hear Becky say, "Tony and I are totally different—night and day different!" That was encouraging to hear since differences often compound over time and strain a relationship to the breaking point.

Their marriage has not been exempt from heartache though. They know how it is to journey through the deep waters of financial problems, health issues, raising strong-willed kids, and working hard to keep a marriage on track. They have experienced many of the challenges marriages face and have come out stronger on the other side.

When I asked them what they thought the key was to finishing well in marriage, they both agreed it was *acceptance* of the other partner. Becky explained further, "It has taken some time, but we fully accept each other now. God has broken us down so much, in many refining stages, that it has finally brought us to this place. We can still be ourselves even as we complement and support the giftings of the other."

Something else they do as a couple caught my attention. Every January the Metcalfs take a retreat where they spend a day in prayer, seeking the Lord's direction for the coming year. They go off by themselves for part of the time and then come back together to share what God has put on their hearts.

One of their goals is for each to identify a theme for the new year. Tony's theme when we spoke was "Confidence in Jesus versus confidence in the world." Becky's theme was "The Father's touch on everything I do." Her inspiration came from a recent study of Michelangelo. Seeing God reaching out to touch the limp hand of Adam depicted on the ceiling of the Sistine Chapel moved her deeply. Tony said, "Our themes are like stakes in the ground that hold us steady and focus our thinking on what God is doing."

Another couple who exemplifies a strong, long-term marriage is Jody and Linda Dillow. They recently celebrated their fiftieth wedding anniversary, sharing that occasion with their four grown children, their children's spouses, and their ten grandchildren. I was curious to find out what they felt was at the heart of their success.

The word they both emphasized was *faithfulness*. According to the Dillows, the top two priorities in marriage are faithfulness to God and faithfulness to your spouse.

Jody said, "A lifelong commitment to faithfulness in these two areas has been the key to our marriage. From there it is also crucial to have friends who are committed to the same values who will walk with you and hold you accountable."

They both acknowledged that staying faithful in today's culture is not easy. Linda shared that the daughter of an overseas missionary couple came to the United States to go to high school. The young woman was surprised when one of her new classmates asked her, "Have you decided who you'll live with when your parents divorce?" The question was an honest one. Sadly, it reflects the attitude held by many young people who see the lack of marital commitment from the adults in their lives.

Jody said that "it's important to live with the end in mind. It's difficult to keep these commitments to faithfulness unless you have an eternal perspective. It has nothing to do with the environment surrounding you. It's much bigger than that."

The Metcalfs and the Dillows inspire us with the knowledge that our marriages can last "as long as we both shall live." Keeping their words of *acceptance* and *faithfulness* at the forefront of our relationships is great advice.

Seventy-Two Years

Can you imagine being married for seventy-two years? I can't, but my grandparents hit that mark. Their relationship illustrated the value of staying faithful to your spouse over a long period of time to allow God's story to be fully written.

Paul and Louise, Pop and Gram to us, epitomized the stable, traditional family we read about from the 1950s. Their home in Southern California was the central meeting place for my family as I grew up.

If I had to identify one area that posed a problem for them, it would be regarding spiritual matters. My grandmother was burdened about her husband's lack of faith in the God she loved. Pop was a man of high morals and was a good provider, but he didn't perceive his need for a Savior. She prayed for him every day of those seventy-two years, but she never lived to see him take a notable step to follow Christ. However, God honored her prayers when he finally affirmed that decision through the help of his grandson—me.

I had flown to California to attend my grandmother's funeral. She had passed away on Palm Sunday, and the memorial service was during Easter week. I went in to see my grandfather, who had suffered several small strokes that had left him in a hospital bed, unable to move or speak. However, he could hear and he knew when people were in the room.

I went in and held his hand. He immediately grew still. I could tell he was listening for my voice. I sensed a prompting from the Lord and said, "Pop, I know you don't like lying in bed, being unable to talk or move around. But do you know that this coming Sunday is Easter? This is when we celebrate that Jesus rose from the dead to give us the promise of eternal life with Him. Do you find hope in that fact?"

I saw a slight nod on the pillow. I thought my eyes were playing tricks on me, so I asked him again a little more directly.

"Pop, that's great. This Sunday is Easter. Do you find hope and comfort that Jesus died for you and rose again to defeat death? That someday you will be with Him in heaven?"

Again there was a slight, but definite, nod on the pillow. There was no mistaking it. I knew that my ninety-four-year-old grandfather had responded to the simple truth of Christ's death and resurrection. Perhaps he had quietly come to that conclusion before, but I was humbled and thankful to the Lord to have been able to experience that moment with my grandfather. I prayed, committing him to his Savior, and then had to leave for the funeral service.

A couple of days later I came back to say good-bye before I returned to Colorado. He was lying in his bed as usual, but my greeting was met with no response. Even a shake to his shoulder couldn't rouse him from his stroke-induced sleep.

I realized that God had opened up a small window of time two days earlier when my grandfather could hear the words of eternal life. I held his hand again and lifted up a prayer of thanksgiving for what had happened previously in that room. That was the last time I saw him before he passed away a few months later.

Seventy-two years is a long time to remain faithful in a marriage and not receive the answer to prayer you desperately wanted. My grandmother finished her life well. She trusted the Lord with her deepest desires, realizing some were not going to be fulfilled in her lifetime. Yet I know she was thrilled to welcome her husband to heaven, knowing her prayers had finally been answered.

Leave Your Spouse to Me

Thinking about a seventy-two-year marriage might seem overwhelming when we are grappling with more immediate problems. We can arrive at those higher anniversary numbers by being faithful in the present moment to work through the troubles that arise with our spouses.

I remember a time when my wife and I were in a difficult stretch as a younger couple. I drove up to the mountains near our home and found a place to park. The view of the valley stretched out below. As I prayed and wrestled with what was going on, I received a strong impression from the Lord that said, "Leave Kathleen to Me! Take your eyes off her and work on your own life. Become a nurturing husband to her and learn My ways."

Ecclesiastes 9:9 was a good reminder for me at this point:

> Enjoy life with the woman whom you love all the days of
> your fleeting life which He has given to you under the sun;
> for this is your reward in life and in your toil in which you
> have labored under the sun.

Here are some statements that God drove into my mind during that time:

> "Keep living with integrity in all things."
> "Honor your marriage vow."
> "Seek the welfare of your wife, for this pleases Me."
> "Don't give up! Stay faithful to Me and My calling in your life."
> "I will add many blessings in the future as you do what I've
> asked."

Those hours away helped shift my attitude and got me back on the right track.

Joining two people together for a lifetime is not an easy task. If our expectations are unrealistic, our partners will disappoint us unless something changes. Frankly, this has been one of the biggest issues that Kathleen and I have had to deal with. We didn't realize our expectations coming into marriage were sky-high. We had a hard time accepting each other's shortcomings. Now we are much more realistic in acknowledging our hurts and imperfections.

Mark Hall, from the band Casting Crowns, wrote about this in a heart-tugging song called "Broken Together." He said, "'Broken Together' was inspired after several conversations I had with friends on relationships. Marriage is tough, and it got me thinking about how we bring a lot of fairy tales to the picture when it comes to marriage. We think, 'This is going to be perfect. We're not going to have any problems.' And then when the problems hit, you don't know where to fit them into your picture."[2]

He wrote with such insight into the marital relationship. Every couple should be required to listen to the recording and consider making it their theme song.

The lyrics say, "Maybe you and I were never meant to be complete. Could we just be broken together? If you can bring your shattered dreams and I'll bring mine, could healing still be spoken and save us?"

There were over two hundred comments posted about this song on Facebook. See if you identify with any of them:

> Florence: Hubby and I just celebrated our 50th Wedding Anniversary … 8 breakups … 6 kids, and even a divorce with a remarriage a year later (we don't even count that anymore) but love prevailed and we are loving away our Golden Years … hang in there, folks. It's worth it.

> Julie: I am recently divorced.… We spent almost twenty years together.… I am only sharing that I do still love him.… Thank you for allowing me to express my brokenness.… Tears.

James: This was our story twenty-two years ago. We were broken together and this week we celebrated forty-three years of marriage. God heals!

Mom: This song is the story of my marriage. I pray every day for God to give us strength to endure the storm our life has been since we got married. I know that God will make things right between us in His time. This song reassures me that it will happen.

An Affair to Remember (or Avoid)

The story of David and Bathsheba is one of the most well-known in the Bible. We are drawn in by this affair between a powerful king and the beautiful wife of a soldier at war. All the passion they enjoyed during those fleeting moments could not compare to the destructive consequences that soon followed. If he were able, David would beg us to avoid his mistake.

David's son, Solomon, wrote most of the book of Proverbs, which teaches us about living with wisdom. It is interesting to consider whether Solomon was remembering back to the tragic affair between his father and mother when he wrote the following:

> Can a man take fire in his bosom
> And his clothes not be burned?
> Or can a man walk on hot coals
> And his feet not be scorched?
> So is the one who goes in to his neighbor's wife;
> Whoever touches her will not go unpunished. (Prov. 6:27–29)

There are important life lessons to glean from the ramifications of David's sexual tryst with Bathsheba. Let's take a closer look at some of them.

As a warrior, David was vigilant to recognize external threats to his kingdom. No nation was able to stand against him as he experienced God's deliverance for Israel multiple times.

Unfortunately, he failed to see a dangerous internal threat that lurked nearby. He left himself vulnerable to face one of the toughest battles of all—maintaining his personal integrity.

David was defeated on the moral field of battle when he compromised God's principles and committed adultery. He experienced the sad consequences set forth in the Scriptures and saw his life spiral out of control from that point forward. His actions led to Bathsheba's pregnancy, deceiving her husband, covering up the affair, the eventual murder of an innocent man, and the death of David and Bathsheba's newborn child not long afterward.

God dispatched Nathan the prophet to confront David over what he had done. The king didn't grasp the magnitude of his error until he heard Nathan's story about a wealthy landowner who killed a poor man's pet lamb to feed an out-of-town guest. David roared in judgment, saying that man should be put to death. Nathan declared, "You are the man!" This broke David's heart, and he was finally able to see the depth of his own sin, which he confessed before God (2 Sam. 12:1–15; Ps. 51).

Two Haunting Verses

Two of the most haunting verses in Scripture appear during Nathan's confrontation with David:

> Nathan then said to David, "You are the man! Thus says the LORD God of Israel, 'It is I who anointed you king over Israel and it is I who delivered you from the hand of Saul. I also gave you your master's house and your master's wives into your care, and I gave you the house of Israel and Judah; and

if that had been too little, I would have added to you many
more things like these!'" (2 Sam. 12:7–8)

David's sin disqualified him from receiving the full blessings that
God had planned for him. The statement "And if that had been too
little, I would have added to you many more things like these!" is a gripping reminder that our future holds unexpected benefits that we can't
foresee today. David had no idea how far-reaching the consequences
of his actions would be when he broke God's commands by sleeping
with another man's wife. Future generations of David's descendants were
negatively impacted. Two of his sons attempted to overthrow him, and
his children suffered moral failure, rivalry, and death.

When reading the story of David and Bathsheba, it's easy to point
out what went wrong—David didn't go to war as he usually did; he was
bored. He didn't avert his eyes; he let his mind go where it shouldn't have
gone. He knew it was wrong, yet he allowed passion to overrule common
sense. He covered up; he denied. We have the benefit of being outside
observers. But what happens when we are embroiled in the drama? An
ensnaring situation can expose us to a fall if we are not ready.

Internal and external threats to our marriages are often subtle. They are
like a prowler quietly checking the doors and windows for entry inside.
Doing the hard relational work with our spouses keeps all the locks in place.

Lord of the Breakthrough

In 2 Samuel 5:20, King David introduced a name of God that is particu-
larly relevant to marriage: the "Lord of the Breakthrough."

At that time, David was the new king of Israel, and the Philistines
were determined to put an end to his reign before it could get started
(2 Sam. 5:17–25). They spread themselves across the Valley of Rephaim
by the tens of thousands. They were the fiercest warriors of the day, and
they dominated the entire region.

Seeing the immense threat facing him, David prayed to God, asking if he should engage them in battle. The answer was yes, so David led his men in the attack. He experienced a great victory over the Philistines as God delivered him from a seemingly impossible situation. That was when David called God "Baal-perazim—the Lord of the Breakthrough," because it described what he saw happen on the battlefield. The word conveys the image of a raging flood of waters that sweeps away everything in its path.

Are you familiar with Lord of the Breakthrough as a name of God? In very specific ways, God can be the Lord of the Breakthrough for you.

This breakthrough by God was so remarkable that Isaiah the prophet wrote about it over 250 years later:

> For the LORD will rise up as at Mount Perazim,
> He will be stirred up as in the valley of Gibeon,
> To do His task, His unusual task,
> And to work His work, His extraordinary work.
> (Isa. 28:21)

Even if we feel stuck and overcome by our present circumstances, it is heartening to read this description regarding how God works. He will use unusual and extraordinary means to provide a breakthrough in our lives.

We have read about the incomparable love of God for His wife, Israel (also for you and me). We've gotten to know Hosea and Gomer, whose marriage overcame huge obstacles to become a living parable of God's love to the world. We learned about the value of acceptance and faithfulness from couples who have been married a long time. The pitfall of unrealistic expectations in marriage can set up couples for big letdowns. However, the idea of being "broken together" can help these couples connect more deeply to each other. The heartbreaking consequences of King David's affair with Bathsheba were presented to caution us about the need to maintain our personal integrity. Then we learned about a memorable name of God—the Lord of the Breakthrough—that provides the hope of divine breakthroughs with the Lord's help in our marital life.

Now we must ask ourselves if we are willing to take the next step toward our spouses and watch God work.

It's very possible that someday our marital relationships will be an inspiration to those following behind. They'll see that God became the Lord of the Breakthrough for us and that they can finish well in their marriages as we are doing in ours.

Moving Mountains Moment

The statue of David sculpted by Michelangelo (1501–1504) was made out of a flawed piece of marble. An earlier artist had begun to work on it but later quit. The large block sat neglected for twenty-five years before it was commissioned again. This time, under the skilled hands of the great master of the Renaissance, the marble came to life. When it comes to moving mountains in our marriages, God has unlimited ways to bring about the shaping we need to be the best husband or wife for our spouse. We may feel flawed or long neglected, but in the hands of our marvelous Creator, a beautiful outcome can result. It may not be an instant fix by divine intervention. It could be the faithful chipping away of the rough edges of our life. What is most important is that we let God do His sculpting work. "But now, O LORD, You are our Father, we are the clay, and You our potter; and all of us are the work of Your hand" (Isa. 64:8).

6

PEBBLE OR BOULDER

Most of us greatly underestimate the impact our lives have on others. We may think it's like throwing a pebble in a pond. Actually, God's plans for us are closer to casting a boulder into the water, with ever-increasing ripples of influence spreading outward. Often we are unaware when those ripples are set in motion.

Nowhere is this more evident than in engaging with our children and family. We are given the opportunity to influence multiple generations. Some have even suggested that each of our lives can have a hundred-year impact.

For an unlikely young woman named Annie, this generational reach was true, although she didn't know it. She lived close to poverty, working as a field laborer picking cotton in Texas during the Great Depression.

Water ripples (iStockphoto, used with permission).

Her husband was fortunate to be hired by a wealthy landowner who needed help planting and harvesting his crops. He and Annie moved onto the property, where they lived in a simple house near the large Victorian home of the owner.

Before long, Annie gave birth to a baby girl named Jane. As the years went by, it became obvious that Jane was musically talented. Annie prayed that somehow her daughter could break free from the cotton fields and pursue an education.

Mrs. Harris, the wife of the landowner, also recognized Jane's abilities. Having no children of her own, she took an interest in Annie's daughter. Soon Mrs. Harris's afternoons were spent pouring her love of art and music into Jane. Something wonderful happened during those days as Jane's musical gifts were developed along with a growing love for God. Annie's prayers were being answered.

When Jane grew up, she started a family of her own. She gave birth to her daughter, Robin, and instilled the same passions she had received years earlier. Robin had three boys and three girls, each with exceptional musical ability. Little did Annie know, as she toiled in those hot fields, that the ripples of her life and prayers would sweep across to her great-grandchildren. She could not have imagined that as a sibling group they would play at Carnegie Hall in New York City or release multiple albums featuring hymns of the faith and classical recordings.[1]

Some might feel that having a four-generation legacy is not possible. And yet the opposite is true. Our lives have the potential to reach across multiple generations. We have only to start setting those ripples in motion. Let's heave that boulder!

Increasing the Impact on Our Families

Jody and Linda Dillow, whom we met in the last chapter, are seeing the ripples of their lives spread across multiple generations of their family. It is rare today for a marriage to reach its fiftieth anniversary. When that milestone was a year away for them, they decided to do something special to celebrate the occasion.

They booked reservations in Lake Tahoe, California, for all their children and grandchildren to join them for a family reunion. A year's worth of planning went into making those days memorable.

Even more important than enjoying fun-filled activities together, Linda shared, "We wanted our grandchildren to realize a marriage can last fifty or more years and plant that idea in their minds. We also knew it would be an encouragement to our grown children who feel the pressures on their marriages like everyone does."

The highlight of the reunion was a unique evening that Jody planned as a surprise. For each of his ten grandchildren, he had written a personalized blessing for their lives. After dinner on the final night, he gathered everyone together. Starting with the youngest, he called each grandchild to come up in front of the family. As the young person stepped forward, Jody spoke the words of blessing he had prepared. He finished by laying his hands on them and praying for their future.

Tears were soon flowing. Hearts had been touched. There's no telling how many generations the words and prayers spoken by that faithful grandfather will influence.

For the ancient cultures of the Bible, speaking blessings over people and laying hands on them held great significance. Something invisible yet very tangible transferred from one person to the next. The Scriptures provide numerous examples that spiritual and even physical outcomes resulted when that transfer occurred.

Paul wrote to Timothy, saying, "Do not neglect the spiritual gift you received through the prophecy spoken over you when the elders of the church laid their hands on you" (1 Tim. 4:14 NLT). The apostle was pointing his young disciple back to remember a pivotal event in his life. How inspiring it must have been for this budding leader to be surrounded by older men of faith who laid their hands on him and spoke prophetic words into his life.

In the Old Testament, the patriarch Jacob realized his death was near and called his twelve sons together. To each he gave a unique blessing, including important admonitions about the son's future. The text describes it this way: "This is what their father said to them when he blessed them. He blessed them, every one with the blessing appropriate to him" (Gen. 49:28).

Jacob waited until the last minute to do this. It's remarkable that he even made it based on what the final verse says about his closing comments: "When Jacob finished charging his sons, he drew his feet into the bed and breathed his last, and was gathered to his people" (Gen. 49:33). He died right after he spoke, which is cutting it very close.

I hope that we can speak such blessings earlier, while we still have time to see the fruit of those words of encouragement. Inspiring our children, families, and others with words from our hearts need not be onetime events squeezed in at the eleventh hour. With a little intentionality we can use a variety of formal and informal occasions for this purpose.

The Count of Monte Cristo

A memorable scene in the movie *The Count of Monte Cristo* (2002) illustrates the power of speaking a blessing over our children. It is Albert Mondego's sixteenth birthday. He is dressed in his finest clothes and seated at the head of a lavish banquet table surrounded by many guests. The high point of the party arrives when the toast is to be given. Sadly, his father is busy elsewhere, so his mother, Mercedes, slowly rises to her feet unsure of what to say. As she begins, the count recognizes her dilemma and stands in to deliver this unforgettable toast:

> Young Albert has made far too much of the assistance I gave him in Rome. When I arrived in the catacombs, I watched as the criminals who tied Albert to a wall, threatened to cut off his finger and send it to his father as evidence of his abduction. [Guests gasp at hearing this.] The boy's reply to all this was, "Do your worst." Life is a storm, my young friend. You will bask in the sunlight one moment, be shattered on the rocks the next. What makes you a man is what you do when that storm comes. You must look into that storm and shout as you did in Rome. "Do your worst, for I will do mine!"

Then the fates will know you as we know you … as Albert
Mondego, the man!

The force of these words to build up the heart of this young man is
obvious. Yet for us, such encouragement doesn't need to be delivered with
the polish of a Hollywood actor. It can simply be a genuine expression
of blessing, affirmation, and counsel to another at the Lord's direction.

After reading this section, someone may come to mind who needs
to hear a word from you. You should schedule the arrangements for that
conversation or event soon while you are thinking about it. Then watch
God show up and work through you to inspire that person.

Jacob's influence played a part in setting the course for future generations and in bringing the Messiah to the world! In ways known and
unknown to him. Four centuries later, Moses continued to speak words
of blessing from God to these same sons, except now their offspring had
multiplied into thousands of people (Deut. 33).

God used Moses to commission Joshua for his new leadership assignment over Israel. In both public and private gatherings, Moses called him
to be courageous and lead the people into the land God had promised
them. During one of those occasions, a significant outcome resulted. We
read, "Now Joshua the son of Nun was filled with the spirit of wisdom,
for Moses had laid his hands on him; and the sons of Israel listened to
him and did as the Lord had commanded Moses" (Deut. 34:9). Joshua
was given divine wisdom through the intentional prayers and laying on
of hands by his mentor.

While Moses didn't wait as long as Jacob did to say his final remarks
to Joshua, death was approaching quickly for him as well. Even though
Moses was 120 years old, the Bible says, "his eyesight was clear, and he
was as strong as ever" (Deut. 34:7 NLT).

Because of his apparent good health, Moses may have been taking
his time transferring the reins of power over to Joshua. He had been

speaking publicly about it, but the Lord urged him to take more decisive action. The text describes the conversation this way: "Then the Lord said to Moses, 'Behold, the time for you to die is near; call Joshua, and present yourselves at the tent of meeting, that I may commission him.' So Moses and Joshua went and presented themselves at the tent of meeting" (Deut. 31:14). Fortunately, Moses responded promptly to the Lord's request and released his responsibilities to God's appointed successor.

Have you blessed the next generation? In profound ways, the Lord will amplify the influence of our efforts as we step out, knowing He has grand plans in store for those we leave behind.

An Unexpected Blessing

Parents may wonder if all the sacrifices they made of love, time, and finances have been worth the investment in their children's lives. My friend Chris Crossan had the chance to find out about this firsthand.

He and his wife, Karen, were missionaries in Turkey when he started experiencing pain in his left shin. When a noticeable bump formed, local doctors were concerned and advised him to return to the United States for tests.

An MRI revealed a stage III sarcoma tumor that was growing inside the tibia bone extending up to Chris's kneecap. It was an aggressive form of cancer that eventually led to the amputation of his left leg above the knee. The surgery brought an abrupt end to a work in Turkey that Chris thought would continue for the rest of his life. The chemotherapy he took damaged his kidneys, jeopardizing his life even further.

In the middle of the crisis, Chris sent out an email to update his friends regarding the status of his health. He closed the letter with this tribute to his wife and children:

How many men have not two or three, but four beautiful daughters—each one of them polished jewels? They are my crown of honor ... and then there is Karen, my lifelong companion. When we sit together for our morning tea, when we laugh together about life's mishaps and pray together for our loved ones, when I gaze at her and am still struck by her beauty, I realize how blessed I am. It doesn't matter whether I live another twelve months or twelve years. On earth my cup overflows, and in the future there awaits an open gate in heaven. I tear up every time I think of that day when I will embrace the one who gave his life for me, and finally be able to talk with him face to face.

When I read those closing words, I was deeply moved. Could I write something like that about my family and then be willing to tell my friends about it? Chris expresses a depth of relationship with his wife and daughters that sets a great example for us.

When they returned to the States, neither Chris nor Karen had a job or a place to live. What they did have were close connections with their adult children. Their eldest daughter, Janelle, invited them to live with her. She told them they could stay indefinitely and decide what to do later.

Chris's medical problems allowed his daughter the opportunity to honor him for having been a great dad. The years of personal investment in her life had borne its fruit and come back to bless both him and his wife.

Broken Relationships

Some of us readily admit to making poor parenting decisions that wounded the hearts of our children. Others rebelled against what they were taught and chose to live life their own way.

Greg and Julie experienced the latter situation. They were committed Christian parents but struggled to maintain a good relationship with their son, Brian. As the teenage years came, Brian grew angry and distant. He would often stay out all night and be gone for days.

It was evident he was using drugs and carousing with the wrong friends. Greg and Julie tried everything they knew to pull Brian away from this lifestyle, but they had no success. He refused to follow any house rules, was untruthful, and lacked true repentance. On multiple occasions he would ask for forgiveness but would fall back into the same behavior. They finally told him he had to move out.

This led to a long season of struggle in a strained relationship. Brian had problems with the law, he couldn't hold a job, and he had no regular place to live. He rejected his early faith in the Lord. It was a bleak picture.

Greg and Julie stayed in contact with Brian as best they could, and years of prayer finally began to show results. Once into his twenties, Brian realized he was on a dead-end road and slowly started to reconnect with his family. They saw him assume more responsibility for his actions and break away from the bad choices of his past.

Taking a calculated risk, Greg offered him a job in the warehouse of the family business. Since he didn't have a car, Brian rode in to work every day with his dad. This gave them time to rebuild their relationship.

Brian went through dramatic changes during the months he worked in the warehouse. He renewed his faith in the Lord, and his life started turning around. He later met Kate, who was a strong Christian, and her influence on him helped to accelerate his spiritual growth.

Fast-forward several years. Brian and Kate fell in love and got married. Later they became the parents of two children. When the time came to dedicate their kids to the Lord, they flew in from another state so Greg and Julie could attend the dedication ceremony.

Brian still works for his dad, but he graduated from the warehouse and is now the main salesman for the company. His relationship with his parents has been restored, and Greg and Julie are grateful for all that God has accomplished.

Struggling in a broken relationship with one of our children is heart wrenching. It can feel hopeless and beyond our reach for repair. Yet if we take the long view and stay connected to them as best we can, we allow God time to show up in each of our lives. Isn't that how God relates to us when we are far from Him? He stays involved and shows His love to us in a variety of ways. Let's hold on to hope as we ask God to mend our hearts and restore our relationships.

Killer Whales and Prowling Lions

When we commit ourselves to finishing well with our families, we must also acknowledge that there is an Enemy of our souls. The first stanza of the great hymn "A Mighty Fortress Is Our God" says:

> *A mighty fortress is our God, a bulwark never failing;*
> *Our helper He amid the flood of mortal ills prevailing.*
> *For still our ancient foe doth seek to work us woe;*
> *His craft and power are great and armed with cruel hate,*
> *On earth is not his equal.*[2]

It's unnerving to think about demonic entities out there with hateful intentions toward us. Jesus said that Satan is a thief who "comes only to

Killer whales moving in (François Gohier Photography, used with permission)

steal and kill and destroy" (John 10:10). We can be thankful that Satan is a defeated opponent because of the death and resurrection of Jesus. Even though we have been given a clear victory over this adversary we call the Devil (Rev. 12:7–11), we should not be ignorant of his schemes.

I sat mesmerized watching a National Geographic special that filmed a pod of killer whales as they relentlessly attacked a large gray whale mother and her calf off the coast of Monterey Bay, California. The gray whale's migration route took her and her calf into dangerous waters along the Pacific Coast where the orcas were waiting to track them.

The killer whales worked as a team, ramming the calf, seeking to separate it from its mother. If that happened, they would force the young whale under the water until it drowned. The mother gray whale continued to fight them off and kept lifting her weakened calf to the surface where it gasped for air. She protected her baby between her huge flippers rolling over as a shield from the hunters. Fortunately, the film footage showed that this particular assault was unsuccessful and the calf was spared.

Killer whales attacking gray whale (François Gohier Photography, used with permission)

A battle like this can go on for hours. If the mother is especially aggressive, sometimes the killer whales will give up. But that rarely occurs.

After watching this coordinated attack against the gray whales, I could see a comparison to the challenges facing families today. What used to be the normal activities of childhood, such as attending school, having friends, or enjoying safe entertainment, now put our children on a dangerous path filled with predators. Similar to the mother whale, parents must be vigilant to protect their children from the dangers lurking in those waters. Sadly, even with great effort, casualties still occur.

The apostle Peter chose a different example from the animal kingdom to emphasize the seriousness of the spiritual battle around us. He wrote, "Be of sober spirit, be on the alert. Your adversary, the devil, prowls around like a roaring lion, seeking someone to devour" (1 Pet. 5:8).

A lion uses stealth, camouflage, and strength to attack its prey. How often have we watched a clueless wildebeest or gazelle wander from the herd unaware of the great predator stalking nearby? The kill that followed was swift and merciless.

How can we grasp the urgency of Peter's warning in this verse?

Imagine if you were hiking near a zoo and received a message that a lion had escaped. How would that change your plans for the day? Instantly, you would be watchful, surveying the surroundings for any sign of the beast. You wouldn't waste any time in moving to safety while constantly being on the lookout for the animal. This is the kind of spiritual intensity Peter was hoping his readers would demonstrate regarding their faith in Christ and awareness of the Enemy.

The apostle went on to write, "But resist him, firm in your faith, knowing that the same experiences of suffering are being accomplished by your brethren who are in the world. After you have suffered for a little while, the God of all grace, who called you to His eternal glory in Christ, will Himself perfect, confirm, strengthen and establish you" (1 Pet. 5:9–10). He was confident that the roaring lion would be defeated by our steady resistance and enduring trust that the Lord would fight for us.

The first epistle bearing Peter's name was written from Rome. He knew that the followers of Jesus were undergoing severe trials throughout the Roman Empire. His words called attention to what was truly important in life. There was no expectation of living a comfortable faith, but rather they lived with confidence that God would meet them in the midst of dire circumstances. Peter pointed them to the resurrection of Jesus, their inheritance in heaven, the protection of God, and the great value of their faith.

Within a year or so after this writing, Nero unleashed a relentless persecution against the followers of Christ. Peter found himself in the center of the storm. Church history indicates that he lived his final years there until he was martyred.

Casualties of the Spiritual Battle

Reading the words of Peter describing our Enemy as a stalking lion or learning how orcas hunt gray whales reveals how daunting the perils are for someone trying to stay on the path to finish life well. Especially while we have an Enemy determined to make us fail.

We've read about individuals who persevered through poverty, bravely faced cancer, and repaired broken relationships. But what about a person who seems to skate by most problems and has it all in life?

My friend Todd spoke with sadness about his mother. Donna was a beautiful woman who had hopes of becoming a Hollywood star. She grew up in a good family with a mother's love that encouraged her to pursue her dreams.

She married young to a handsome fellow named George, believing he was the ticket to making her wishes come true. He bought her nice clothes and worked hard to get her the possessions she wanted.

But it wasn't long before Donna's dreams came crashing down around her. The first setback occurred with an unexpected pregnancy that ruined any chances for stardom. Her body was not the same after the pregnancy, and she blamed George for the predicament she was in. Unfortunately, Donna did not have the qualities of her mother and felt stuck in a maternal role. Another baby came along, and the difficulties of family life compounded.

George worked tirelessly to provide for the family. He was successful but still fell short of Donna's dreams of wealth and prestige. Over time, he began to stay longer at the office to avoid the growing difficulties at home. When present at the house, he did all he could to keep the peace, even serving Donna meals on a tray in the bedroom, where she preferred to eat alone. The door remained closed for hours, keeping him and the children out.

Todd shook his head as he thought about growing up in that kind of family. He didn't ever remember having a good relationship with his mother or hearing her say she loved him. His father was the opposite and expressed his love often to Todd and his sister. Sadly, George endured terrible verbal abuse from Donna during their married life but somehow found a way to respond to her with care.

I asked Todd how someone could end up as his mother had. He thought a moment, then said a single word: "Unforgiveness." The implications of his mother's dreadful attitude have rippled across Todd's family, and they have had to work hard to counter them.

Donna had a good home—she had a loving husband, two great children, five wonderful grandchildren, and a comfortable life where her every need was met—yet she was consumed with unforgiveness. How tragic! Somewhere along the way it appears that the roaring lion stalked and captured his prey.

Tamarisk Tree

Even though there are mountains that block the way on our journey to finish life well with our children and families, Scripture is quite optimistic about us succeeding in this area. Jesus said that these mountains could be thrown into the sea with a little faith in Him on our part (Matt. 17:20). We also read the frequent repetition of "fear not," "be not afraid," "trust in the Lord," and "be strong and courageous" throughout its pages. The emphasis repeatedly directs us to rely on God's strength to overcome any adversity. While we might struggle in these areas, He doesn't! And He freely offers us help and hope along the way. His extraordinary plans for us are going forward, unhindered in "perfect faithfulness" as we read in Isaiah 25:1.

While we may have head knowledge that this is true, God desires that we tangibly grasp His involvement in our lives, proving the reality of His promises. Therefore, He will give us ample opportunities to grow in our dependence on Him.

A clear example of this is found in two fascinating verses in Genesis 21.[3] They illustrate how Abraham literally got his hands dirty to make a statement of profound trust in God. It's especially poignant since he had not taken possession of the land that had been promised to him. Here is what these verses say:

> Abraham planted a tamarisk tree at Beersheba, and there he called on the name of the LORD, the Everlasting God. And Abraham sojourned in the land of the Philistines for many days. (Gen. 21:33–34)

What is described in these verses has particular significance for moving mountains and finishing well in the context of our children and families. It might not be obvious at first glance, so let's look more closely at what Abraham did.

First, he planted a tamarisk tree. Why would he have done that? What was special about this particular tree? Digging up the arid soil to bury a seed was tantamount to stating, "This land is mine, and God will be true to His promises." Here is what Bible historian and teacher Ray Vander Laan said about the tree:

The shade of a tall, slow growing tamarisk (salt cedar) tree is a blessing in the desert. The small feathery leaves of the tamarisk excrete salt crystals which absorb the little moisture in the air. As the salty water droplets evaporate from the leaves in the heat, the air beneath the tree is cooled. Desert travelers and shepherds prize this tree. The Bedouins say, "We plant tamarisks for our grandchildren," apparently meaning "Because they grow so slowly and last for a long time, we will not enjoy them, but our grandchildren will."[4]

Tamarisk tree (iStockphoto, used with permission)

Beersheba was also a distinct location in which to grow this tree. It represented the southernmost boundary of the Israelite monarchy in later years. Abraham chose the farthest place he could find to mark out the land he believed that God would give him. When he stood and looked to the north, the land lay before him in a vast expanse. Ray said it was like saying, "I believe You, God! I am going to do something in faith (plant a tree) that will bless my grandchildren and great-grandchildren. When they enjoy its shade, they will realize how great a land the Lord gave them."

To drive home the point of this verse, Ray asked his students, "Did you plant a tamarisk tree today? Did you do anything today that will outlive yourself and bless others for years, decades, and centuries down the road?" Those are profound and visionary questions. How would you answer them?

After Abraham planted the tree, the text says he "called on the name of the Lord [Yahweh], the Everlasting God." He was boldly stating, "God, I absolutely trust You to fulfill Your promise to me because that is the meaning of Your name, Yahweh—God of the Promise!"

He had to live by faith in the gritty reality of waiting for God's timing to come. Verse 34 says, "And Abraham sojourned in the land of the Philistines for many days." We might think that "many days" meant just a few years. That number would be totally underestimated because Abraham's sojourn was actually one hundred years!

He left his home in Haran at God's command when he was 75 years old (Gen. 12:4) and died when he was 175. That is a long time to wait for the promise of God to be realized!

Abraham never saw the fulfillment of God's pledge during his lifetime (Gen. 12:7; 25:9–10).[5] That fact never caused him to doubt what the Almighty had told him. He knew it would take place—someday.

In honor of his exceptional life, the divine text gives him one of the few "finishing well" verses found in the Bible:

> These are all the years of Abraham's life that he lived, one hundred and seventy-five years. Abraham breathed his last and died in a ripe old age, an old man and satisfied with life; and he was gathered to his people. (Gen. 25:7–8)

Here are three things that Abraham did that we can also do to live a life that finishes well and sees the mountains moved:

1. Abraham planted a tamarisk tree. Do something for others that will outlive your life as a demonstration of your faith in God.
2. Abraham called on God. Stay close to God in all that you do.

3. Abraham waited for God's timing. Be confident that God's purposes will be perfectly fulfilled in your life. Don't give up!

The stories of Annie; Jody and Linda; Chris and Karen; Greg, Julie, and Brian; Moses; and Abraham all give us hope that God is working through our lives to accomplish His purposes. They all gripped tightly to their faith and saw the Almighty show up in surprising ways.

In each of their situations, you could say they both planted a tamarisk tree and cast a large stone into the water. The future shade of their tree and the ripples of their influence have greatly benefited or will greatly benefit their children, grandchildren, and great-grandchildren. That is the kind of legacy we, too, can leave, and it is core to a life that finishes well.

Moving Mountains Moment

If you plan carefully, it is possible in a single day to summit three fourteen-thousand-foot peaks in the Rocky Mountains of Colorado. The alpine weather is unpredictable with snow and freezing temperatures possible even in the middle of summer, but Mount Missouri (14,067 feet), Mount Belford (14,197 feet), and Mount Oxford (14,153 feet) are grouped together in such a way that allows this achievement to be done. When it comes to our children and families, these close relationships can be wounded, causing groupings of mountain-like barriers to exist. God does not want us to lose heart but to trust Him as we seek to conquer the relational mountains that appear too difficult to climb. He will walk with us on the steep trail and guide us to the top. This is what we will hear on the path: "Behold, I am the Lord, the God of all flesh; is anything too difficult for Me?" (Jer. 32: 27).

UNEXPECTED FRIENDS

As our children got older, the number of cars in our family grew to four, and those vehicles rotated regularly in the repair shop. I spent a lot of time there and eventually got to know Carl, our mechanic.

He was rough around the edges at first impression. His clothes were oil stained, and grease seemed permanently embedded in the skin of his hands. Yet I found that he was honest and went out of his way to help those in need, often staying late to finish the work.

I'd hang out and chat with him occasionally while he was doing repairs. Sometimes on a Saturday morning I'd bring him a coffee and sweet roll.

I remember inviting him for a bite to eat after he got off work. He agreed, and over hamburgers I learned more of his story.

"Carl, tell me about your family. Are your parents still living?"

"No, they're both gone. I have a sister who lives in town with a couple of kids. Haven't seen my older brother in a long time. He's homeless and lives under a bridge somewhere."

I was sorry to hear that. He commented that he would try to find him every so often and sometimes succeeded. However, he hadn't been able to motivate him to get off the street.

What he said next shocked me.

"I saw my father die when I was twelve years old."

Again, I expressed how sorry I was and told him I couldn't imagine how he coped with it. I asked him what happened and he shared more.

"We were having a picnic at the park. He climbed high up into a large tree and got out on a branch, showing off a little. He wasn't being careful enough, lost his grip, and fell to the ground. The ambulance came. They said he broke his neck. He died at the hospital the next day."

The conversation continued back and forth about his dad for a while longer. He had trusted me with personal information that I knew he didn't share often. I thought, *Lord, Carl has had such a rough life. He needs to know You. Open the door for a chance to talk more with him about You.* We finished dinner, and I drove him to his apartment.

I discovered that even though he was a mechanic he didn't have a car. He had had his license revoked for drunk driving and was waiting for the restriction to be lifted. Our relationship grew to a friendship over time.

Then during one visit to the repair shop, I noticed that a new mechanic was on duty. I wondered what had happened to Carl. When I asked about him, I learned that he was in jail. He'd pushed his luck too far one night and was caught driving again under the influence. The court gave him a fourteen-month sentence as a repeat offender.

I had never visited anyone in jail before. After arriving for my first appointment, I found out they limited conversations to video conferences. The viewing room was large with seats scattered in front of about thirty numbered monitors. Crowded around most of them were women and children talking with men in orange jumpsuits. Carl looked tired as he came onto my small screen. He was doing all right and just counting the days until he could get out.

Over the months in the repair shop and during Carl's incarceration, I shared my faith and encouraged him to trust in the Lord. After a year, he was released into a halfway house. My visits could now be in person, and he was given a little more freedom.

Finally, I decided the time had come to ask Carl to take an important next step. While we sat in my car, talking, I asked him if he was ready to commit his life to Jesus.

Why was I shocked when he said yes? The Lord had prepared his heart, and I led him through a simple prayer of salvation. That decision opened up the chance to get him a Bible and to meet weekly to study what it meant to be a follower of Jesus. I still remember how he tried to carefully turn those thin new pages with his calloused hands to look up various verses.

I had no idea that God would bring Carl to Himself using our friendship as the connecting point. It was encouraging to see God at work in this man's heart.

My relationship with Carl was unexpected. It grew over time. If we are open to it, God will expand the influence of our lives so we can interact with people we never thought possible. If we allow Him, the Almighty will take us into uncharted territory as we extend His love to those beyond our circle of friends. We need to develop spiritual sensitivity so God can use us with the individuals we cross paths with every day.

Chris Crossan (introduced in the last chapter) provides a dramatic example of this. He and his wife, Karen, served as teachers in Turkey for nearly two decades. Their purpose was to represent Christ through the classes they taught to children and adults. Even though the people there were harder to reach with the gospel, a handful of the men Chris got to know were aware that he was a follower of Christ, and they wanted to learn more.

One such man was named Jamal. He was a Muslim who genuinely sought the truth. He was happily married with a two-year-old daughter, whom he loved dearly. He and Chris met each week to discuss matters of faith. Jamal asked probing questions about the life of Jesus and struggled to understand the concept of forgiveness, which was foreign to his religion. Over the subsequent months their friendship deepened and more of Jamal's questions were answered.

Chris remembers Jamal coming to him and thoughtfully stating that he had made his decision to follow Jesus. He desired to be baptized and commit himself to his new Lord. Chris was both thrilled and troubled because he knew the severe price Jamal would pay. In strict Islamic cultures, converting to Christianity would mean estrangement from his family and community with the possibility of receiving a death sentence. They discussed this choice at length, including the consequences that were sure to come. Jamal understood and was later baptized in a small ceremony.

Following Jesus in a Heartbreaking Situation

For a while, all seemed to go well, and Jamal grew rapidly in his faith. He had the joy of a new believer, and the change was evident in his life. Others soon noticed, and he shared honestly about the decision he had made.

Before long, though, heartbreaking events started to happen.

When Jamal's father-in-law heard about his conversion to Christianity, he flew into a rage. He ordered his daughter and granddaughter to leave Jamal immediately and move back in with him. Jamal's wife knew her husband loved her, but culturally she had to obey her father.

Jamal's uncle and father-in-law put out an order for his death. The village was on alert trying to find him to carry out the "honor killing." Jamal fled to Istanbul and hid in a friend's bakery, where he worked for nine months and slept in a roach-infested basement, grieving over the loss of his wife and daughter.

Back at the village, Jamal's father-in-law forced his daughter to divorce Jamal and marry another man. When word of it came to Istanbul, it broke Jamal's will to live. He tried to take his life with an overdose of drugs, but someone found him in time and rushed him to a hospital, where his stomach was pumped. His life was spared.

Jamal's faith held firm after that. He studied the Scriptures and knew that God had not forgotten him. Chris wept when they met and Jamal recounted all that he had suffered. They prayed fervently that God would intervene and use the tragedy of these events for divine purposes.

Jamal continued to work at the bakery until he received some startling news. Hundreds of miles away the new husband wanted nothing to do with Jamal's young daughter. The family sent a message that he could come pick her up. He was overjoyed at the chance to see his daughter again.

Not long after that, the uncle died, and his wife's family canceled his death warrant. They said he could come back to the village and live. He returned cautiously, fearing he was walking into a trap. Remarkably, the furor over his conversion to Christ had blown over. He was reunited with his daughter. They are together now, and Jamal continues to follow his Savior.

As Chris shared this story with me, I had to hold back tears as the significance of Jamal's situation hit me. We sat in silence for a few moments. Chris added that on the subway home, after speaking with Jamal, he had cried out to God, wondering if he had done the right thing. Was it worth all the heartbreak and anguish that had taken place? Quietly, he received confirmation in his heart that if the question had been posed to Jamal, he would have answered with a resounding yes.

Compassion for Those We Meet

To love others beyond our circles of family and friends, sometimes we need to view people in a more compassionate way. Too often I forget that the different (and sometimes strange) people I encounter in public are made in the image of God. They have tremendous worth in God's sight.

Peggy Noonan, columnist for the *Wall Street Journal,* shared some insightful observations that apply to loving our neighbors. As a Washington insider, she lived an elite life far from the day-to-day struggles of the average person. She talked about a transformation that occurred in her thinking about the people she encountered during her day:

> Here's something I thought of in a new way.... Most of the human beings on earth spend most of their short time here in a way that is dictated by money. This is not true of everyone, but so many of us are doing with our days things that are different, sometimes radically so, from what we'd like to be doing. You're a toll collector who wants to act, or you're a teacher who really wants to paint, but you're doing what you do because that is the job the world will pay you to do. And it takes money to live.
>
> Here's the thought that came to me in a new way. When you think about this, you realize that people are so gallant to accept what is and not become bitter or enraged; and so many are kind and humorous and cheerful in spite of the tyranny of money, the bane of life on earth. We are surrounded by the heroic cheerfulness of the average person. It is all around us. We're not moved enough by it.[1]

Changing the way we view people who are outside of our social or economic circles can open up doors of influence in their lives. It may not mean befriending your local car mechanic and building a long-term relationship with him. It could be as simple as showing kindness to the woman standing behind the counter at a convenience store or speaking a word of encouragement to the man who cuts your grass or the custodian who keeps your office clean. Perhaps your word will lead to a deeper relationship that the Lord will use to touch their life.

After hearing a message at church about stepping out in faith, my wife got a call from one of her best friends about an idea. "Why don't we take tacos to the homeless Tuesday night?" asked Susie. Kathleen remained quiet for a moment, caught off guard by the question. "Taco Bell has a ninety-nine-cent special, and we can each take a box and hand them out to whoever we can find," Susie continued enthusiastically.

When Tuesday arrived, Kathleen, along with her friends Susie and Curt, headed out on their new mission. Loaded up with tacos, they walked toward a group of homeless men and women whose eyes brightened at the sight of the food. They were warmly welcomed by that little gathering of people who exist on the outer fringe of society. The conversations that ensued lasted over two hours and even concluded with everyone holding hands in a circle of prayer. Kathleen came home exhilarated by the experience.

There was such a positive response to the evening that they decided to make a return trip the following week. Again, the visit went well. Soon these unknown people had names paired with stories of troubled pasts—Tom and his dog Little Racer, Jerry, Dan, Ernie, Sonja, Charlie and Laura who had a tiny baby, and others who came and went.

It turned into a weekly event. Word soon spread among the homeless that they should come to "Taco Tuesday." One August evening during that time, over forty-eight homeless people stood in a line, waiting their turn to get a taco. When they saw Kathleen and Susie arrive, a couple of the men ran over to the car to help take the food back to the picnic tables. This was the largest group yet, and the food ran out before everyone was fed. But those who didn't get a taco were offered first turn at the fruit cobbler Susie had made. No one seemed to complain; they were glad to get something on their plates.

During this time, Kathleen met Sonja and had to decide if she was going to get more involved. She found out that Sonja was sixty-seven and had quickly spent or lost her welfare money, which put her on the street. It became obvious that Sonja was struggling with physical and emotional challenges. Kathleen sensed that the Lord wanted her to help further.

At the top of Sonja's list of needs was getting her cat back from a pet-boarding service. Kathleen drove Sonja over to pick up her cat and worked to get her affordable monthly payments to cover the charges that had accrued. She also helped her set up a bank account to manage the government assistance checks that often got lost.

As Kathleen, Susie, and Curt reflected over their months of involvement with the homeless on Taco Tuesdays, they realized God had shown up in unexpected ways. They had no idea that taking tacos to needy people in a park would open up so many doors of ministry.

You Can't Be a Christian

Tony and Becky Metcalf are another couple who chose to step beyond their comfort zone to be Jesus's hands and feet to others. They hosted a home Bible discussion and established an unusual prerequisite for those who could attend—non-Christians only. They thought a discussion based on the book of Acts would be a great way to introduce people to Jesus and show how people's lives were changed as a result of faith in Him.

Invitations went out to people they knew at the swim club where their kids took lessons. Neighbors were invited, along with others in their circles of acquaintances.

The discussion had no formal agenda aside from reading what the Bible said and enjoying an engaging conversation. When the night arrived, they were pleased that six couples came. Some wives attended alone and later brought their husbands.

By the time the study concluded, Tony shared that most everyone had become followers of Jesus. Without any pressure and in the context of friendship, God had touched the hearts of those who had participated.

When I talked to Tony recently, he was on the highway, hurrying back to Colorado Springs from a business trip in New Mexico. He would return just in time to meet with seventeen men he was mentoring in the Scriptures. The group would be waiting for him at Panera Bread at seven o'clock that evening. Their ages ranged from twenty-six to fifty-three. Tony said he pushes the guys to dig into the Bible because that is where we encounter Jesus. They are currently going through 2 Corinthians, which is new territory for most of them.

One of the men who started coming each week is an ex-gang member. With his tattoos and tough image, he does not fit the stereotype of a follower of Jesus. But when you see his smile and hear him speak, you quickly realize he is serious about Christ and growing in his faith.

For over thirty-five years, Tony has quietly lived out what he believes is his calling to come alongside men of all ages and backgrounds to mentor them in the Lord. He talks about his own experience of never having a father who was involved in his life or expressed love to him. He said, "I guess you could say my calling is to redeem the lack of having a close relationship with my dad by being a father figure to those who need one in their lives."

Tony's life has impacted hundreds of men over the years. Many of them have shared that he was closer to them than their own fathers. One man gave Tony a letter that read, "Thank you for being like a father to me. I love you." While Tony never heard his dad express love to him, he hears it regularly now from the men he mentors.

Many of the guys who meet with him respond to his challenge to start a group of their own. As a result, countless Bible studies have spun off from Tony's group. For Tony, seeing a man take this next step of faith to reach others is one of the most rewarding parts of his mentorship ministry. He said, "Now I have both physical grandchildren and spiritual grandchildren!"

When asked about finishing well, Tony commented, "Life is not about me; it's more about serving others. Living out the calling God has placed on my life gives me such joy. My identity and life are wrapped up in what Christ is doing in me."

Tony's wife, Becky, experienced the pain of fatherlessness too. She describes being a little girl and finding out one day that her father was gone. He never came back. He deserted his wife and five daughters, leaving them penniless and scraping to survive.

In the midst of this tragedy, Becky recalls that her mother was resourceful and worked hard to provide for their needs. Since they had little money for entertainment, she would bundle up the girls on the weekends and drive them to beautiful locations in the Rocky Mountains. During those walks in the alpine forests and meadows, Becky discovered "an amazing transcendence of comfort." She found that healing came to her heart by exploring the land and taking in its beauty. The mountains became her sanctuary, where she experienced God's love.

Becky's unique ministry today was shaped by watching how her mother celebrated life and transformed their humble circumstances into memorable moments. She explained, "My mother fostered the art of celebration like no one else I knew. Despite heartbreaking difficulties, she had a love for life that rubbed off on all of us girls. She was also extremely generous in helping others while not having much herself. Her life made an indelible imprint on mine."

It's obvious that the creative genes of this talented mother were passed down to Becky. Twice a year in Denver and Colorado Springs, Becky's ministry is to present an extraordinary Four-Course Tea and Art Salon. She combines art, biography, history, faith, storytelling, and delicious food within an exquisite dining environment.

Every event sells out, attracting a wide audience of individuals, including many who do not share Becky's faith in Jesus. Her winsome way of pointing people to the Lord is woven throughout the presentation. She believes that God has called her to represent Him through artistry and beauty.

Here is a short excerpt from one of Becky's elegant invitations. It will give you a feel for the creative way in which she expresses her ministry. The topic she chose for this event was a study on the life of Michelangelo:

Elizabeth Metcalf
presents
"Sacred Servant of Pietra Serena"
featuring the exquisite works of
Michelangelo
Among the most exalted artists in all of history.

It is our honor to invite you to our
Sculpture Garden Four-Course Tea and Art Salon.

Lilies will surround you in this late Springtime Tea
as we immerse ourselves in "The
City of Lilies—Florence."

We will share the story of a calling
as difficult as the white
Carrara marble he loved to fashion and cut.
While Michelangelo was chiseling with his hands,
a Master's Hands were chiseling him,
always taking him deeper into life's mysteries.

One of the most important subjects
Michelangelo would portray
again and again was his reverence
for motherhood which
we will unfold to you throughout the courses.

My wife and I have attended several of Becky's special events and always come away inspired to be more passionate about following Jesus.

She truly experiences the joy of using her gifts to further the purposes of heaven. When I asked Becky about what it meant to finish well in life, she said, "Every drip and drop of my calling is to learn and create beauty for the Lord." She added, "I want my Father's touch on everything I do."

These stories are powerful examples of what can happen when we take the risk to love our neighbors. In small and large ways, they illustrate how God shows up when we step out in faith for Him. Have you thought about using your gifts more fully to serve others on behalf of Jesus? You have much to offer!

"My Father is glorified by this, that you bear much fruit, and so prove to be My disciples" (John 15:8). This verse inspires us to consider using our gifts in a much greater way. As we go about life this week, let's keep our eyes open for those the Lord brings across our paths. He just might have divine appointments waiting for us!

Moving Mountains Moment

A rancher was trying to figure out how to keep his cows from wandering away across an open prairie. A barbed-wire fence would be too expensive to construct. Instead, he decided to drill a well for the cattle. His problem was solved as the herd stayed close to the source of water. If we aren't sure how to connect with individuals outside our circles of relationships, expressing God's love is the equivalent of drilling a well. People respond to those who show a caring interest in their lives. Barriers come down when that occurs. "Jesus answered and said to her, 'Everyone who drinks of this water will thirst again; but whoever drinks of the water that I will give him shall never thirst; but the water that I will give him will become in him a well of water springing up to eternal life'" (John 4:13–14).

ASSIGNMENTS

"What if God crushed me in order that I could meet your needs better?" When I heard David Brown make this statement, I marveled at his attitude. He spoke to me from a wheelchair.

David was a gifted counselor who had relocated his family to Colorado Springs a couple of years earlier to join the counseling team at the Navigators ministry headquarters. He was a marathon runner and outdoorsman. One fateful evening as he rode his mountain bike home after work to enjoy the beauty of the Garden of the Gods park, with its huge sandstone ridges rising hundreds of feet, his bike momentarily left the trail and got caught in some deep sand. The front tire stopped abruptly, and David went flying over the handlebars. He landed on his head and broke his neck at the C1 vertebra. This is called the "hangman's break," and few survive it.

Providentially, someone who had emergency medical training came upon him right away and watched over him until paramedics could arrive. David went from a marathon athlete to a quadriplegic in the blink of an eye. His world was forever changed.

Medically speaking, David is a miracle for not only surviving but also regaining some movement in his body. As we sat and talked, I watched him slowly bring his arms up to feed himself and even stand for short periods of time. Once he had recovered, he returned to work and had a full schedule of counseling appointments. However, what impresses me most about David is his indomitable spirit and willingness to surrender completely to whatever God wants to accomplish in his life.

I visited him again about a year after he made that remarkable statement to me to see how he was doing. It was coming up on the fifth anniversary of his accident.

He talked about his journey, which had not been easy. "God has met me in the deepest areas of my suffering and continues to speak into that. I've had to let go of things I can't do any longer, but not everything! I realize how important perseverance is. It is a passionate patience in the Lord where I am determined not to give up."

Then he said something else that stuck with me. "We must be on a God hunt. That means actively looking for what God is doing around us and being alert to what He will do next." Time spent with David always stretched my faith.

As we neared the end of our visit, he asked if I would follow behind him for his walk across the room. *He could walk?* I looked on as he locked his wheelchair, then very slowly pushed himself up to a standing position and grabbed a walker. Then, amazingly, he started taking steps every four to five seconds and walked about twenty feet through the office area. After he sat back in the wheelchair again, I rolled him to his office, where we prayed together and said our good-byes.

Ephesians 2:10 says, "We are His workmanship, created in Christ Jesus for good works, which God prepared beforehand so that we would walk in them." God has met David in the darkest places of the human soul. His counseling reflects this as Navigators' staff from around the world come to take his marriage courses and receive personal mentoring from him.

Jesus stated in John 17:4, "I glorified You on the earth, having accomplished the work which You have given Me to do." On the cross He knew that every single thing required of Him had been fulfilled: "After this, Jesus, knowing that all things had already been accomplished, to fulfill the Scripture … said, 'It is finished!' And He bowed His head and gave up His spirit" (John 19:28, 30).

Each of us has assignments from the Lord to complete. Determining what they are should be foremost in our thinking. They should drive our actions and interactions. During a leadership team event, I listened to my colleague Michele Wilson share the extraordinary story of Benaiah.[1] He was King David's bodyguard and a fearsome warrior. She read from 2 Samuel 23:20–21, "He also went down and killed a lion in the middle of a pit on a snowy day. He killed an Egyptian, an impressive man…. He went down to him with a club and snatched the spear from the Egyptian's hand and killed him with his own spear."

Could an assignment be any more difficult than that? Go down into a deep pit. It's freezing cold, slippery, and hard to see. Then you are to kill a ferocious lion that is waiting there to devour you! For your next assignment, your opponent will be even bigger, a skilled assassin, possessing a better weapon and bent on killing you as well.

We are going to learn a lot more about this remarkable man named Benaiah in chapter 11. King David chose him out of every warrior in the nation to be his personal protector, the head of his bodyguards. Benaiah offers us a striking example of someone who fulfilled his assignments to the utmost, even at great personal risk.

Robbing God of His Glory

In contrast to Benaiah, we're often so anxious about our circumstances that we limit ourselves to what we can accomplish in our own strength. It's too frightening to rely on God's power and intervention. What if He doesn't show up?

When this is our mentality, we are actually robbing God of His glory. We don't allow Him to demonstrate His miraculous power on our behalf because we're afraid. How many of us never see God show up because we won't risk anything that pushes us beyond our natural capacity to resolve a situation?

One of the clearest examples in Scripture of this mind-set is the story of Gideon. We find him in Judges 6, hunkered down in a pit (a sunken winepress), beating out some wheat in order to have a little food for his family. He was fearful of discovery by the Midianites, who had oppressed Israel for seven years.

God sent an angel to Gideon who greeted him in this way: "The LORD is with you, O valiant warrior" (Judg. 6:12). Despite this statement about his character, Gideon saw only the problem. He thought God had abandoned him and no longer did the miracles that he had grown up hearing about. He said, "If the LORD is with us, why then has all this happened to us? And where are all His miracles …? But now the LORD has abandoned us and given us into the hand of Midian" (v. 13).

The angel overlooked his response and gave him a huge assignment: "Go in this your strength and deliver Israel from the hand of Midian. Have I not sent you?" (v. 14). Gideon heard what the angel said this time but couldn't believe it. His shortcomings and excuses were at the forefront of his mind. He said, "My family is the least in Manasseh, and I am the youngest in my father's house" (v. 15). He was looking only at his own abilities—small, weak, and of no consequence—and ignoring God's power to use him.

The angel continued a third time despite Gideon's disbelief and said, "Surely I will be with you, and you shall defeat Midian as one man" (v. 16). God's presence was promised and victory was ensured to such an extent that it would seem as if Gideon defeated his enemies by himself without the help of any army.

There is a striking contrast between how God sees us and how we see ourselves:

> God saw a valiant warrior; Gideon saw his weakness.
> God promised His presence would go with Gideon; Gideon thought God had abandoned him.
> God promised victory over a terrifying enemy; Gideon saw his lowly position and shortcomings.

As the story unfolded, Gideon confronted his fears and took the first steps of action in response to what God had told him to do. He quickly discovered that everything he had heard was true. The Midianites were soundly defeated, but in an unconventional way (three hundred men with trumpets and pitchers against thousands of soldiers) so that God would receive credit for the victory.

Hebrews 11 is called the "Faith Hall of Fame," where the greatest examples of faith in God are recounted. You know who made it on the list? Gideon did in verse 32! He overcame his fear and low assessment of himself to experience the joy of watching God show up on his behalf.

Timothy

Timothy was a young disciple of the apostle Paul. While he was determined to follow Christ, he experienced a great deal of fear. He struggled with feelings of personal weakness and doubt.

Paul wrote him two letters to encourage his heart and strengthen his faith. In 2 Timothy 1:7, we read, "For God has not given us a spirit of timidity, but of power and love and discipline." Paul was concerned for his young follower and did what he could to help Timothy overcome his fears.

We learn something noteworthy about Timothy that is recorded at the very end of the book of Hebrews. It reads, "Take notice that our brother Timothy has been released, with whom, if he comes soon, I will see you" (Heb. 13:23). Timothy finally overcame his anxieties to the point where he willingly faced recrimination and imprisonment for his faith in Christ. When he was released from jail, he didn't hold back from spreading the gospel wherever he went. The writer of Hebrews thought it important to add this fact about him to the sacred text.

Serving God's Purpose in Our Generation

Acts 13:36 records this about the life of David: "For David, after he had served the purpose of God in his own generation, fell asleep." David had no idea what God was up to when he was called from the sheep pastures as a young boy and anointed by Samuel the prophet in front of his brothers (1 Sam. 16:11–12). It took David years before he was able to see how all the pieces fit together after God had placed him as king over Israel (2 Sam. 5:12).

Another man who was unknowingly being prepared for an assignment from God was Jim Downing. He is the oldest living Navigator who served with the ministry since the days of its founder, Dawson Trotman. Jim turned 101 years old in August 2014.

During his twenty-four years in the navy, he was present at the bombing of Pearl Harbor. Later he became the commander of a large ship during the Korean War, tackling what he said were "potentially disastrous missions to do the impossible."

Early in his military career, Jim met Dawson, who had invited a number of sailors over to his house for dinner and a Bible study. It would be another year before Jim put his faith in Christ. As he grew spiritually under Dawson's influence, Jim wondered, *What does commanding a ship have to do with the Great Commission?*

Dawson soon asked Jim to quit the navy and join him at the Navigators. On the weekend he was to discuss Jim's new ministry role, Dawson drowned trying to save a young girl who had fallen into a lake.

The ministry was plunged into crisis, and Jim was called on to run the newly purchased Glen Eyrie Conference Center. Jim said, "Those years of commanding the USS *Patapsco* in Korea gave me the ability to help guide the ministry of the Navigators for three years. That ship proved to be the greatest preparation possible for what I was going to face."

Jim went on to serve the Navigators for twenty-seven years in numerous executive roles, including chairman of the board of directors. Following his formal work, Jim continued to speak and write on behalf of the ministry. Into his late nineties, he still traveled to between six and eight college campuses per year, encouraging students to commit their lives fully to the Lord's plans.

No "Human" Explanation for Success

"There should be no *human* explanation for the success of your ministry." When I heard this statement, it pushed me to do some serious thinking about my service to the Lord. Was I depending on the Holy Spirit to fulfill the divine purposes of heaven through me? Or was I grasping at my own efforts to get the work done for the kingdom?

In 1 Samuel 9, we are introduced to a man named Saul, who later became the first king of Israel. As a young man, he met Samuel the prophet and said, "Am I not a Benjamite, of the smallest of the tribes of Israel, and my family the least of all the families of the tribe of Benjamin?" (1 Sam. 9:21). He sounded a lot like Gideon, although he seemed to possess genuine humility in the beginning.

Unfortunately, after Saul became king, his pride grew, and he believed his successes were due to his own strength and abilities. He also admitted to Samuel that he feared the people and listened to the crowd's voice instead of God's (1 Sam. 15:24). He was given many opportunities to follow the Lord. However, Saul never broke free of his pride, and his thirty-two-year reign ended in disaster when he committed suicide to avoid falling into the hands of the Philistines (1 Sam. 31:4).

I had a conversation with Dr. Joe Wheeler on the topic of pride. He is an author of over eighty books and is probably best known for his *Christmas in My Heart* series. I received a letter following our time together in which he wrote:

I'm convinced that God spends a disproportionate amount of His time on just one of our character traits: Pride. For until we win modest victories over it— none of us ever completely gains the victory over it—God can do little with us. Once we're gloating over being pre-eminent in anything (size of church, ministry, business, etc.), the devil has the inside track on us. Pride has the seeds of its own destruction built into it. But once we ascribe all glory to God, and sublimate self, God can finally use us in special ways.[2]

A great question to ask ourselves is "What is there about my life and ministry that cannot be explained apart from God?" We read in John 15:5, "He who abides in Me and I in him, he bears much fruit, for apart from Me you can do nothing." It's not about us and our plans, but God's plans and what He wants to bring about in our lives.

Each of us has assignments from the Lord of Hosts to accomplish in our generation. As in the cases of David, Benaiah, Gideon, Timothy, David Brown, and Jim Downing, those assignments will be discovered over time and require boldness from us to fulfill them. We must avoid the trap of pride and instead watch expectantly for all that God can accomplish through a life that is humbly surrendered before Him.

Moving Mountains Moment

A blank sheet of paper can feel like an imposing mountain if we don't know what to fill in as our assignment from the Lord. It's possible we make it too rigorous by looking for divine direction to clearly intersect our lives. Could it be more like what theologian Frederick Buechner said: "Vocation is where our greatest passion meets the world's greatest need"?

God created us with desires, interests, and aptitudes that work together to accomplish His purposes. Over time, we'll find our blank sheet of paper gets filled up as we seek to honor Him in all that we do. "Who is the man who fears the LORD? He will instruct him in the way he should choose. His soul will abide in prosperity, and his descendants will inherit the land" (Ps. 25:12–13).

PART THREE

THE CORNERSTONES

Living Out the Six Principles for Moving Mountains

9

HEROIC INVISIBILITY

Over one thousand people had gathered to commemorate the retirement of a distinguished man of God. His ministry had spanned fifty years, reaching individuals across the globe. Speeches would be made, songs sung, and videos shown highlighting his many accomplishments.

Before the ceremony began, I saw my friend Phil, who told me that it was his last day of work. I was surprised and then saddened to learn he had multiple sclerosis. He was going on medical disability that would mark the end of thirty-five years in professional ministry.

After we finished our conversation, I watched as he slowly took a seat at the rear of the auditorium. The contrast between the ends of these two careers struck me. Both were men of God observing their final days of lengthy ministry service. One's achievements were obvious and celebrated on a brightly lit stage. The other, though just as deserving of recognition, went unnoticed in a seat near the back.

Don was another man in the audience that day. He watched the ceremony from the confines of a wheelchair on the far aisle. Over twenty years earlier, doctors had removed malignant tumors from his spine to save his life. The surgery left him paralyzed from the waist down.

After Don recovered, he continued to practice as a licensed marriage and family counselor. Every day he took appointments and answered calls on a ministry hotline to assist those in desperate need.

He continued to offer caring counsel to hurting people into his seventies. Those he spoke with on the crisis line never knew the depth of his suffering, but they benefited from his advice, which had been forged in the "crucible of the chair," as he would say. All this took place in a back office far from the spotlight.

Taking calls for long stretches of time gave Don terrible muscle cramps. Yet he pushed through the pain and kept at his counseling ministry until he physically couldn't do it any longer. Health issues finally forced him to step back from the work he loved and did so well.

The office sits empty now. Most people who walk by wouldn't know about the thousands of lives that were blessed by the man in the wheelchair who occupied that small room for so many years.

Heroic, but Invisible

Phil and Don have something in common. They are living in heroic invisibility, which is one of the cornerstones of a life that finishes well.

Heroic invisibility means honoring our vows to the Lord regardless of any recognition from the world. It is living a life of integrity before an audience of One.

This idea is expressed in Matthew 6:4: "So that your giving will be in secret; and your Father who sees what is done in secret will reward you." God sees the many sacrifices we make, though everyone else often overlooks them. These invisible acts of service are fully rewarded in heaven.

This is contrasted by the celebrity culture we all live in, which is obsessed with notoriety and the quest for personal attention. Everyone craves to have a moment on center stage.

Honoring your marriage vow day after day won't make the headline news. Showing up for work to keep food on the table or spending sleepless nights caring for a sick child won't score any recognition points either. Few will pat you on the back for your faithfulness through thick and thin. No one will know all that you have done, except One. And He is the only One who counts.

Many invisible heroes are recorded in Hebrews 11. They were described, in part, by the following: "They went about in sheepskins, in goatskins, being destitute, afflicted, ill-treated (men of whom the world was not worthy), wandering in deserts and mountains and caves and holes in the ground" (Heb. 11:37–38). We will never know their names, but we stand on their shoulders.

"Men of whom the world was not worthy" implies how exceptional these individuals were in the eyes of heaven. Nothing on earth could come close in value to what they represented. The caves where they lived were far from the glow of the world's limelight.

Many people struggle with the implications of this point. It's one thing to nod our heads in agreement as we read a passage from Hebrews that describes unknown individuals who suffered terribly because of their faith in God. But it's another thing to personally experience it.

While we might not be scourged, be stoned to death, or live in a cave, we do have to pay a price for living lives of faithfulness before the Lord. Most men and women, husbands and wives, parents and grandparents will be confronted by feelings of invisibility, the lack of external affirmation for their caring deeds, and the lonely burden of quiet suffering along the way.

As with Phil and Don, we have the opportunity to live fulfilled lives, knowing that invisibility on earth really means high visibility in heaven.

Nazareth

As the public ministry of Jesus was beginning, people referred to Him as "Jesus of Nazareth" from the region of Galilee. The Pharisees were unimpressed by the area and asked that a search be made to see if any prophet would arise from there (John 7:52). When Philip elatedly told Nathanael that they had found the Messiah, the question came back, "Can any good thing come out of Nazareth?" (John 1:46).

Interestingly, the city of Nazareth is not mentioned in the Old Testament. It was located in southern Galilee about seventy miles north of Jerusalem. As a small, out-of-the-way place, it did not have a good reputation. Yet Jesus carried that descriptor with His name for the duration of His ministry and mentioned it again when He spoke to Paul on the road to Damascus (Acts 22:8).

The Almighty picked an obscure (invisible) place to live in humility as He emptied Himself fully for our sake. His radiant glory was hidden from the eyes of the villagers even while His words continued to uphold the entire universe.

Measuring on Eternal Scales

We live in a world where values are skewed out of proportion. We have no idea what is important according to heaven's standards. God has a different way of seeing things than we do. Significant earthly achievements are often insignificant when weighed on His eternal scales. The Scriptures describe it this way: "Behold, the nations are like a drop from a bucket, and are regarded as a speck of dust on the scales" (Isa. 40:15).

Let's weigh some things on heaven's scales:

Honoring your marriage vow weighs a lot in heaven but is light on earth.

Living with integrity weighs a lot in heaven but is light on earth.

Serving God faithfully weighs a lot in heaven but is light on earth.

Achieving great wealth tilts the scales on earth but isn't a speck of dust in heaven.

Gaining a position of power tilts the scales on earth but isn't a speck of dust in heaven.

Being successful in worldly pursuits tilts the scales on earth but isn't a speck of dust in heaven.

My dear friend Sami lives in Cairo, Egypt. When his mother, Sara, passed away, he sent out a tribute about her to all his friends. She lived to be eighty-six years old. Here is a part of what he wrote:

She guided me to know the Lord and to abide in the faith. She taught me to accept challenges, endure difficulties, maintain integrity, and live an abundant life with little.... She taught me that aging does not mean losing hope in life, but should serve as a determination to live for Him all the days He entrusts us with.... My mother inspired me in countless ways.... Her simplicity and love are perhaps her greatest legacy.

Sami's mother never held a position of power or public influence, never enjoyed the abundance of material wealth, and never received outside recognition for devoted service to her family or her faithful ministry to the Lord. But she lived a big life by heaven's standards—one of heroic invisibility.

Significance of Genealogies

When reading the Scriptures, most people skip over the chapters containing the lengthy genealogies of people. Who are these people with hard-to-pronounce names from strange places anyway?

Some of the chronologies record the lineage of the Messiah that God preserved over millennia to provide a Savior to the world. Quite an unusual cast of characters forms this privileged group.

However, I believe there is another reason the Bible preserves all the names of these individuals in long lists. It is to emphasize how personal God's relationship is with mankind. Paul talked about this idea when he spoke to the Greeks of Athens in Acts 17:26: "He made from one man every nation of mankind to live on all the face of the earth, having determined their appointed times and the boundaries of their habitation."

While we may feel invisible to the world around us, we are highly visible to God. Look at the details recorded by the writer of 1 Chronicles about the lives of many people long forgotten by the world. It gives interesting insights into who they were:

Nimrod—a mighty one on the earth (1:10).
Peleg—the earth was divided in his days (1:19).

Sheshan—had no sons, only daughters. He had an Egyptian servant named Jarha and gave his daughter to Jarha in marriage (2:34–35).

Jeconiah—the prisoner (3:17).

Jabez—more honorable than his brothers, he asked God to bless him, enlarge his border, guide him, and keep him from harm. God answered his requests (4:9–10).

Joab—a craftsman (4:14).

Bithia—daughter of Pharaoh (4:17).

Linen workers who lived in Beth-ashbea (4:21).

Potters who lived in Netaim (4:23).

These descriptions demonstrate that God knows the details of our lives. He knows our names, our families, and our work; and He placed us in the nations, cities, and neighborhoods where we live. He recognizes our daily acts of faithfulness as well. Jesus emphasized this point when He said, "Indeed, the very hairs of your head are all numbered. Do not fear; you are more valuable than many sparrows" (Luke 12:7).

Do Not Grow Weary

When living in heroic invisibility, we must acknowledge that it gets tiring. We are in the midst of a spiritual marathon, and exhaustion can set in.

Long-distance runners describe getting a second wind that overcomes their fatigue, giving them new strength. That reality also holds true in spiritual matters. Isaiah wrote, "Yet those who wait for the LORD will gain new strength; they will mount up with wings like eagles, they will run and not get tired, they will walk and not become weary" (40:31). Paul urged the believers in Thessalonica, "But as for you, brethren, do not grow weary of doing good" (2 Thess. 3:13). He made a similar statement to the Corinthian church, reminding them that "your toil is not in vain in the Lord" (1 Cor. 15:58).

If you find yourself needing a second wind to move ahead in heroic invisibility, the Scriptures provide the way forward. Here are some important recommendations the Bible gives us:

- Revere the Lord (Ps. 128:1–4).
- Be strong in the Lord (Eph. 6:10).
- Be faithful (Matt. 24:45–47).
- Endure hardship (2 Tim. 2:3).
- Stand firm (Eph. 6:11, 13–14).
- Stay in the race (Heb. 12:1).
- Finish the course (2 Tim. 4:7).

While you continue on the journey, keep your eyes open for others living in heroic invisibility. If you meet one of these hidden heroes, take a moment and share a few words to cheer the person on. Maybe someone will do the same for you.

Moving Mountains Moment

The Scriptures remind us that planet earth is not our permanent home. We are actually "strangers and exiles" here as the book of Hebrews states. The apostle Paul told the Philippians in Greece that they were "citizens of heaven." This is important to keep in mind as we struggle with feeling invisible and unvalued by the world. It is a mountain that God can move when we realize He is planning a great celebration for us when we arrive at our true home in heaven! Until then, God says we are of incredible value to Him and "the very hairs of [our] head are all numbered" (Luke 12:7).

10
FAMOUS IN HEAVEN

The complement to heroic invisibility is the idea of being famous in heaven. Heroic invisibility looks at the earthly implications of living for the Lord. Fame in heaven offers us a glimpse of how our deeds are regarded in eternity. The meaning of *famous* is not the same as the meaning of fame on earth. It is the celebrated recognition of an individual who is living according to the standards of heaven.

The book of Hebrews describes it this way: "Since we have so great a cloud of witnesses surrounding us … let us run with endurance the race that is set before us" (12:1). When we think our lives are insignificant and invisible, we forget something very important. There is a heavenly stadium filled with those who have gone before us—our families, our friends, and the great saints of old who are cheering us on. We are told the events unfolding in our lives are so remarkable that "angels long to look" at them (1 Pet. 1:12).

Ancient Stadium of Aphrodisias

One of the most well-preserved stadiums of the ancient world is found in Aphrodisias, a city named after Aphrodite, the Greek goddess of love. It is located along the southwest coast of modern-day Turkey.

I was fortunate to travel there on a study tour with Ray Vander Laan. Ray is a gifted Bible historian, teacher, and author of the That the World May Know DVD series. He makes the Scriptures come alive by exploring the original locations of biblical events and describing what an eyewitness would have experienced.

The stadium in Aphrodisias could seat thirty thousand people. Ray led us down to the floor where the athletes had competed. We were transported back in time, imagining the crowds shouting support for their favorite champions.

Ancient stadium in Aphrodisias (author photo)

As our group gathered in front of the place designated for the emperor, Ray asked us, "Who is in the heavenly stands cheering you on?" Around the circle different names were mentioned. I thought of my grandmother Louise Peppin, who followed Jesus for over seventy years. She often prayed for me, and I knew she was somewhere in those celestial seats. If that question were posed to you, who would come to mind?

If we could hear those immortal crowds, I imagine their voices would be declaring loudly, "You can do it! Keep going! Don't give up!" With every spiritual victory we gained, they would rise to their feet in thunderous applause.

To help the nation of Israel remember when God accomplished something extraordinary in their midst, the people would pile up stones in commemoration. Those "standing stones" lasted for generations as testimonies to what the Almighty had done.

After the Jewish people miraculously crossed over the Jordan River into the Promised Land, twelve large stones were removed from the riverbed, and the leaders set them in the middle of their camp. Here is what Joshua said at that time:

> Let this be a sign among you, so that when your children ask later, saying, "What do these stones mean to you?" then you shall say to them, "Because the waters of the Jordan were cut off before the ark of the covenant of the LORD...." So these stones shall become a memorial to the sons of Israel forever. (Josh. 4:6–7)

The groups Ray has led into that stadium over the years have created a pile of standing stones in recognition of the people who encouraged them to run the race for the Lord. I walked over and added a rock on behalf of my grandmother. I could imagine her smiling in heaven to hear me speak her name.

Author by standing stones (author photo)

Our Time Is Short on the Field of Competition

Psalm 103:15–16 says, "As for man, his days are like grass; as a flower of the field, so he flourishes. When the wind has passed over it, it is no more, and its place acknowledges it no longer." The book of James builds on this idea by stating, "You are just a vapor that appears for a little while and then vanishes away" (4:14).

Looking across those worn and cracked marble seats, I realized my time on the field of competition would pass by quickly. How seriously was I taking the race? Was I jogging slowly along, or was I running hard?

I prayed in that moment, asking God for the courage to hold nothing back and to give it my all. A phrase came into my mind that described what I was feeling: *to the greatest extent possible, to the best of my ability.* That's what I intended to do.

Standing on the floor of that ancient arena, Ray spoke passionately to us about our races. He shouted like a coach, "Let us run, run, run!" Then he told us he had one more thing to do—and he took off running around the track! After our initial surprise, we chased after him. Some helped the slower ones along, and others could only walk. Those who had already reached the finish line cheered the ones coming behind. Eventually, each person made it across. It was a beautiful picture of God's race.

Someday, at the end of the course, we will take our seats in the heavenly stands and join in the cheering. Perhaps a loved one will add a standing stone somewhere in memory of the race we ran for the Almighty.

Big in Heaven, Small on Earth

Generally, earth takes notice when something is impressive or receives a lot of fanfare. Heaven's measures are counterintuitive. By heaven's standards, small acts often exceed the big ones in eternal significance.

Jesus taught His disciples about this while sitting in the treasury observing how people were contributing to the temple. Large sums were being poured in publicly by the rich, but with little personal sacrifice.

When a poor widow arrived and quietly dropped in two small copper coins, Jesus exclaimed that she had given more than everyone combined (Luke 21:1–4). Heaven took notice of this extravagant gift that amounted to only a tiny fraction of an average day's wage. Jesus also stressed the significance of a single cup of water given in His name as having an eternal reward. "For whoever gives you a cup of water to drink because of your name as followers of Christ, truly I say to you, he will not lose his reward" (Mark 9:41).

No one would think that two tiny copper coins and a cup of water would rank that high. But according to heaven's measurements, they do.

This is a spiritual paradox. How can the small things on earth actually be the big things of heaven? You're famous there if you are a faithful husband or wife, father or mother, son or daughter, grandfather or grandmother, friend, or servant. For each role, we must keep our ears tuned to hear those stadium crowds cheering us on.

The painting called *Man in a White Silk Waistcoat* captures this notion. The artist was an Englishman named Joseph Highmore (1692–1780), who created the work around 1745.

Man in a White Silk Waistcoat (Bridgeman Art Library, used with permission)

The pose of the man is called the "teapot" stance and was used to denote individuals of high status and wealth. What's unusual is the clothing of the fellow. The white waistcoat, black breeches, and dark blue woolen coat were worn by middle-class professionals, not the aristocracy. The modest wardrobe is accented with a tiny gold cufflink, wrist ruffles, and a large powdered wig. The man must have paid a considerable sum for a well-known artist such as Highmore to produce this aristocratic painting. And he did his best to look the part.

Even with all his efforts to memorialize himself, history does not know his name. It remembers only the painter with a description of the outfit worn that day! Had the fellow considered what it meant to be famous in heaven, perhaps he wouldn't have bothered posing for the expensive portrait at all. Instead, he could have used the money to help others in need.

Many years ago I read a poem called "The Children and Sir Nameless" written by Thomas Hardy (1840–1928). He was an English poet and novelist who wrote extensively about British society. He observed people's constant grasping for recognition and significance. Yet for all that striving, weren't these just fleeting achievements that would be soon forgotten? Wasn't there anything more important to pursue in life? Much like the man in the painting, the subject of Hardy's poem is a nobleman who wants his *mightiness* to be remembered for perpetuity by a huge statue. He accomplishes his goal (so he thinks), and the statue stands for a long time. Yet later he is forgotten, and the effigy on its pedestal ends up taking up too much room in the church. So it's taken down and made a part of the floor, where schoolchildren (whom he despised) kick off his nose and name, ultimately winning out over him!

As you read the poem, think about how it relates to being famous in heaven in contrast to pursuing acclamation on earth. The words are in old English, but the message still comes through.

The Children and Sir Nameless

Sir Nameless, once of Athelhall, declared:
"These wretched children romping in my park
Trample the herbage till the soil is bared,
And yap and yell from early morn till dark!
Go keep them harnessed to their set routines:
Thank God I've none to hasten my decay;
For green remembrance there are better means
Than offspring, who but wish their sires away."

Sir Nameless of that mansion said anon:
"To be perpetuate for my mightiness
Sculpture must image me when I am gone."
He forthwith summoned carvers there express
To shape a figure stretching seven-odd feet
(For he was tall) in alabaster stone,
With shield, and crest, and casque, and word complete:
When done a statelier work was never known.

Three hundred years hied; Church-restorers came,
And, no one of his lineage being traced,
They thought an effigy so large in frame
Best fitted for the floor. There it was placed,
Under the seats for schoolchildren. And they
Kicked out his name, and hobnailed off his nose;
And, as they yawn through sermon-time, they say,
"Who was this old stone man beneath our toes?"

Both men sought to be immortalized, one in paint and the other in stone, yet both went nameless and forgotten in the end. Did they settle for the accolades of earth when they could have had cheering crowds in heaven's stadium? Only God knows that answer.

If a painting were to be made of our life today, would it feature a large self-portrait? Or would it display images of more eternal significance?

Armed with the knowledge from these stories, we have the opportunity to rearrange the priorities of our life according to what's treasured in heaven. There is still time to paint over our self-portrait and choose better things, because the colors are not yet dry.

Be encouraged! While the copper coins or cups of water we offer during our lives may not tip the scales much on earth, they tip them significantly on eternity's side. The heavenly crowds are cheering us on to run our race for the Lord of Hosts. Can you hear them shouting your name? Being unknown on earth yet famous in heaven is not a bad trade-off! It is the right perspective to have as we press on to live a life that finish well.

Moving Mountains Moment

We need to think more about heaven. The more prominent it becomes in our minds, the less room we have for the cluttering notions of the earth. If we could wear specially designed glasses made in heaven that filtered everything out except what was important there, what would we see? How would it change the way we view the world? Bob Pierce, founder of World Vision, best captured what it might look like when he said, "Let my heart be broken with the things that break the heart of God." Try putting on those heavenly glasses this week and see what appears. You may find a mountain that God wants to remove so your priorities can better align with what He wants to accomplish through your life. "Seek first His kingdom and His righteousness, and all these things will be added to you" (Matt. 6:33).

11

DECADES, NOT DAYS

The *Mona Lisa* by Leonardo da Vinci is one of the most famous paintings in the world. Da Vinci began the work in 1503 and took about four years to complete it. The painting is a masterpiece of composition and technique created by one of the greatest geniuses of the Renaissance.

Only recently has the *Mona Lisa* revealed some of her most treasured secrets. Through advanced X-ray technology, French researchers discovered that Da Vinci applied up to thirty layers of transparent glaze on her face. Each layer of glaze was between one and two micrometers thick; in comparison the average width of a human hair is eighty micrometers. The technique required months for each layer of glaze to dry.

Mona Lisa (Bridgeman Art Library, used with permission)

The result of this painstaking effort was a stunning achievement of artistry. No brushstrokes appear on the luminescent face that still captures people's hearts five hundred years later.

A process far more intricate is under way in our lives. Instead of layers of glaze, we have layers of experiences and years that are being laid down under the careful direction of our heavenly Father. His hands use every situation to shape our character and deepen our integrity.

Different Views of Time

The process of building character takes a lifetime. We tend to think in days about our development while God thinks in decades (or an entire life!). There are far-reaching implications regarding these differing views of time.

We often hear people say they are waiting on God. They have prayed for months or years about something, and the answer still hasn't come. While that poses a difficult challenge, there may also be an ironic twist mixed into it— while we are waiting on God, He is often waiting on us! It takes more time than we realize to develop the integrity and character required to shoulder His future assignments.

Oak tree (iStockphoto, used with permission)

It's like the difference between growing a lilac bush or an oak tree. A lilac grows rapidly, displaying fragrant blooms in a variety of colors.

By contrast, a little acorn germinates under the surface of the ground unnoticed.

In fact, the odds are stacked against that tiny acorn, as only one in ten thousand grows into an oak tree. When that does occur, the tree can easily live for two hundred years and grow to one hundred feet tall. Many animals and birds find refuge among the branches that are dense with leaves that stay green year round. The wood is hard and strong with intricate patterns in the grain, making it desirable to use for furniture, flooring, and paneling.

Moses

As a younger man, Moses thought he was ready to rescue his people. He saw an Egyptian beating a Hebrew slave. Seeing no one around, he killed the Egyptian and buried him in the sand. The next day he saw two Hebrews fighting and questioned them about it. They asked if he was going to kill them too. Moses realized his murder had become known so he fled into the desert.

He didn't understand that forty years would elapse before he was prepared to return, to do what only God could accomplish—rescue His people from slavery. Moses went from a prince of Egypt to a humble shepherd in a remote part of the Sinai Peninsula to begin his training program.

Moses's timing was way off. He thought he was qualified to deliver Israel (Acts 7:25), when actually he needed decades of preparation. It was during that lengthy season in the wilderness that Moses came to know his God. He also learned about herding sheep so he could be a trusted shepherd of the Jewish people.

At eighty years of age, Moses was finally ready for his expanded assignment. As he led his flock near Horeb, the mountain of God, he saw an amazing sight—a burning bush that was not consumed by the fire. When he turned to go see it, the Lord called to him from the center of the fire (Exod. 3:2–10; 7:7).

After some divine convincing, Moses was willing to overlook his own weaknesses and instead trust in God's promise to deliver His people. As he retraced his journey across the desert, Moses must have had flashbacks to his anxious escape from Egypt. The steps he made before, as a fearful man on the run, were now replaced by confident ones, willing to face the same peril with God on his side.

Moses went on to lead the nation of Israel out of bondage just as God had promised at the burning bush. He watched the Almighty use him to take ten plagues to the land. It is intriguing to note that each of the plagues targeted one of the gods that the Egyptians worshipped.

The Israelites were miraculously released from captivity and journeyed into the wilderness (Exod. 12:31–42). Unfortunately, it wasn't long before they lost confidence in God's ability to take care of them and, sadly, rejected Him (Num. 14:34–35). This breach of faith resulted in wandering forty years in the desert until that doubting generation died off.

By this point, Moses was 120 years old. He got to see the Promised Land from a distance, but he couldn't go in himself (Deut. 34:1–8).

His life encompassed three seasons of four decades each. When he was a young prince of Egypt, the idea of needing to wait forty years to be ready for God's greater assignment never crossed his mind. And having to endure another forty years in a wasteland with a rebellious people was beyond comprehension. Moses's sense of God's timing was off by only eighty years!

Eight Decades of Preparation

While waiting eight decades is a long stretch of time, here are the names of some other people whose assignments came during later stages of life:

> Abraham was one hundred when Isaac was born (Gen. 17:17).
>
> Sarah was ninety when she gave birth to Isaac (Gen. 17:17).

Jehoiada was eighty-three when he launched his plan to rescue Judah from evil Queen Athaliah (2 Chron. 23:1–10).

Jehoshabeath was eighty when she rescued the baby Joash, future king of Judah (2 Chron. 22:11–12).

Caleb was eighty-five when he asked for the hill country of Israel (Josh. 14:10–12).

Anna the prophetess was eighty-four when she held Jesus in her arms (Luke 2:36–37).

Simeon was an old man when he held Jesus in the temple (Luke 2:25–35).

Most of us are on decades-long journeys in becoming ready for God's expanded assignments. However, as with the people listed, we don't know what our future roles might be. Until that moment arrives, we have a huge inventory of minutes, hours, and days to spend on whatever God puts in our paths to do. We are given many preparatory tasks (probably in the thousands) that forge our character and further our development. Growing from these training sessions is crucial for our spiritual progress. We should not diminish their importance or the service to God they represent.

God's Purposes Are Discovered

In discussing the principle of "decades, not days" with my friend and colleague Ron Wilson, he shared an important insight. He told me, "God's purposes for our lives are discovered, not created. Revealed, not self-determined. It isn't something that we can force into existence based on what we think should happen."

For Ron, discovering God's purpose took an unexpected turn. After undergoing medical tests to diagnose unusual symptoms he was experiencing, the results came back indicating he had Parkinson's disease. The news arrived like a bombshell, leaving him to question whether God had anything more for him to do.

As we discussed his medical condition, Ron asked, "Why did God allow me to have Parkinson's at the peak of my life? I now take 140 pills a week to counteract the effects of the disease." He then answered his own question for my sake, saying, "God gives us a specific set of weaknesses through which we can glorify Him." I had never thought of it in those terms before.

Ron acquired Parkinson's in his early fifties and is now living with it in his sixties. While his professional work assignments have changed, his ministry impact has expanded far beyond what it was before. His life is packed full with individuals and groups that seek his counsel or want him to speak. Whenever I have the chance to see him, I am usually busy taking notes to remember the insights he shares with me.

Some may believe that the opportunities for increased service to God have passed them by once they reach their fifties and sixties. Yet each of us is on a decades-long training process leading to the next divine assignment. Perhaps, as with Ron, that new endeavor might arrive in an unexpected way.

Benaiah's Journey of Preparation

I am intrigued by the life of a relatively unknown Bible character named Benaiah. We met him briefly in chapter 8 when we discussed our unique assignments from the Lord. Benaiah's story illustrates this idea of "decades, not days."

The details of his life are spread across 2 Samuel, 1 Kings, and 1 Chronicles. Piecing the three narratives together provides some fascinating highlights about his story, including the fact that he was King David's personal bodyguard. Let's look more closely at what stands out:

> He was a valiant man (2 Sam. 23:20).
> He was a skilled warrior (2 Sam. 23:20–21). He killed a lion
> in a pit on a snowy day and killed a seven-foot-tall Egyptian
> assassin with the Egyptian's own spear.

He was over King David's bodyguards (2 Sam. 8:18) and served a long time in this role (2 Sam. 20:23).

He served in a lesser role (2 Sam. 23:23).

He served as the third commander of the army (1 Chron. 27:5).

He was promoted as commander of the thirty mighty men (1 Chron. 27:6).

He stood for what was right no matter what the cost (1 Kings 1:8).

He served King David at great personal risk (1 Kings 1:32–37).

He was promoted over the entire army by King Solomon (1 Kings 2:35; 4:4).

Even though Benaiah never attained the status of the "three mighty men" (1 Chron. 11:24–25), his decades of integrity and perseverance awarded him the warrior's greatest prize—a promotion to commander of the army. Over the years he rose through the ranks from being an individual warrior to attaining the highest military post. Now all the mighty men and soldiers were under his authority. He served both King David and King Solomon.

The accomplishments of his life are exemplary. But behind the achievement is something more significant—the heart of a servant and follower of God. As you read through this list of the attitudes he exemplified, do any stand out as needing improvement in your situation? (I admit to identifying several areas in my life!)

- Demonstrated a servant's heart
- Gave his best in any job
- Was willing to serve in a lesser role
- Served faithfully in one job for a long time
- Showed courage in each situation
- Kept his fighting skills sharp

- Developed his intellect
- Maintained his integrity
- Trusted God completely

Waiting Decades in Exile

Two more largely unknown biblical characters give us further insights into this concept of "decades, not days." When was the last time you heard a sermon about Zerubbabel and Jeshua from the book of Ezra? Both of these men were born in Babylon during the seventy-year exile of Israel.

When Cyrus, king of Persia, conquered the Babylonians, he allowed the Jewish people to return to their homeland (Ezra 1:1–3). Zerubbabel and Jeshua were part of the leadership team that led the initial group back to Jerusalem.

One of the first things they did was to build an altar to the Lord (Ezra 3:2). How did they know how to do that, having lived most of their lives in Babylon? It was a unique skill set not taught in the pagan temples there. They learned those techniques by studying with older Jewish captives who passed the knowledge down.

After establishing the altar and its daily sacrifices, they started building the second temple to worship the God of heaven. Huge foundation stones were set in place with large beams of wood laid into the walls (Ezra 5:8). Great care was taken, and the work was succeeding. But again, how do men held captive learn how to construct a temple on such an enormous scale?

It is obvious Zerubbabel was not idle during his decades of exile. He was not defeated by finding himself in a foreign land against his will. Developing a wide range of leadership and construction skills would not have been easy, but he found a way to do it.

During his prolonged hiatus in Babylon, Zerubbabel kept his faith in God strong, studied the law of Moses, learned how to build things, took on leadership responsibilities, demonstrated courage, and maintained close friendships. He found that the years of waiting and preparing in Babylon were worth it as he led the rebuilding effort for the temple in Jerusalem.

Where do you find yourself now? Are you in a lengthy period of preparation, like an acorn germinating in the ground? Or are layers of fine glaze being added slowly to your portrait? Maybe you feel as though you're in exile. Or perhaps, like Zerubbabel, the long wait is over and you are actively serving in a new assignment for the Lord. No matter what your current circumstances may be, God is doing a deep work in your life and continues to prepare you for His assignments.

While living through this process can be difficult, we should allow the season of development to run its full course. It's possible that our greatest influence and impact will come during our second half of life. It might even happen when we are eighty years old!

Moving Mountains Moment

Business books have popularized the ten-thousand-hour rule. The rule states that if someone has accumulated that amount of time in any one field he or she will have mastered the essentials to achieve success. There is the understanding that it takes an extended season of preparation to reach this level. Why should we think any differently when it comes to our spiritual development and readiness for God's assignments? If we are patient, the mountain, representing delayed expectation, will be removed by the Almighty after He has completed our training process. At that point we will experience the joy of serving Him in an expanded way. "Wait for the LORD; be strong and let your heart take courage; yes, wait for the LORD" (Ps. 27:14).

12

BE READY

The Adventure Grand Slam is the ultimate in extreme outdoor events. It includes climbing to the top of the highest peaks on the seven continents, plus skiing to both the North and the South Poles. Only forty people in the world have done it.

One of the summits is Mount Everest, which is the highest in the world at 29,035 feet. Sometimes mountaineers are so intent about reaching the top that they forget it is only the halfway point of the journey. The return trip is nearly as hard as going up. Did you know that most mountain-climbing deaths occur on the way down when the climbers have exhausted their energy?

> The descent on Everest's summit ridge is harrowing—it's a 10,000-foot drop on one side and an 8,000-foot drop on the other. You have to descend the infamous Hillary Step, a forty-foot spur of near-vertical rock and ice at 28,740 feet, and make it back down to the South Col at 26,300 feet, so you better have enough reserves—both in your oxygen tank and in your body. Otherwise? You'll die. You don't ever want to fail and wonder if the outcome would have been different had you only been more ready.[1]

It is obvious that rigorous training is required for this type of expedition. Years of preparation go into achieving a goal of this magnitude, especially when lives are on the line.

However, when we move from ascending natural mountains to spiritual ones, the scenery becomes much more obscured. In the temptation of Jesus in the wilderness, "the devil took Him to a very high mountain and showed Him all the kingdoms of the world and their glory; and he said to Him, 'All these things I will give You, if You fall down and worship me.' Then Jesus said to him, 'Go, Satan! For it is written, "You shall worship the Lord your God, and serve Him only"'" (Matt. 4:8–10). How prepared do we need to be to face the same tempting offer?

I came face-to-face with my lack of readiness to scale a spiritual mountain when I heard the following question: "If God was looking for someone to use on an important assignment for the kingdom, would you be the one He'd choose, given your present attitude, behavior, and choices?" That inquiry hit me hard as I thought about it. Honestly, I had to admit, *No, I wouldn't be the one to pick. I'm not ready.*

When I looked closer at the reasons, what I found wasn't pretty. I tended to play it safe. Even my son, Brooks, noticed this and asked me one time, "Dad, why do you always hold back?" I mumbled out some kind of lame answer. I didn't realize it was that obvious, but he was right. At the core, I didn't believe that God would show up so I operated as if every outcome depended on me. Because of that belief, my risk tolerance was low and my confidence levels were lacking.

I got tired of living such a defeated life and determined things were going to be different with God's help. (I shared more about this on p. 61.) One of the verses I held on to during this time was Isaiah 41:10, which says, "Do not fear, for I am with you; do not anxiously look about you, for I am your God. I will strengthen you, surely I will help you, surely I will uphold you with My righteous right hand."

The ideal situation finds us ready when God's next assignment knocks on our door. As we read in the last chapter, it can take decades of training to be prepared for that hour.

When Your Hour Comes

The Scriptures refer to an "hour" in several ways. Typically, it is used to mark a point of time. It can also mean "a duration of time": "I also will keep you from the hour of testing" (Rev. 3:10). But the hour we are referring to here is the arrival of a specific, defining moment.

Jesus was very aware when His momentous hour had come as noted in the following verses:

> It is enough; the hour has come; behold, the Son of Man is being betrayed into the hands of sinners. (Mark 14:41)

> The hour has come for the Son of Man to be glorified. (John 12:23)

> Jesus knowing that His hour had come that He would depart out of this world to the Father, having loved His own who were in the world, He loved them to the end. (John 13:1)

> Father, the hour has come; glorify Your Son, that the Son may glorify You. (John 17:1)

The hour that Christ faced represented the colossal culmination of the plan God had set in motion before the ages began. No power in heaven or on earth could hinder the flawless execution of these divine purposes in Christ.

Think of the millions of variables that were in play with the events leading up to the climactic hour of the betrayal and crucifixion. Thousands of individuals played small and large roles in fulfilling what took place. Any one exception could have potentially derailed it.

What if Judas had changed his mind after the Last Supper and not led the mob to the garden of Gethsemane?

What if the chief priest had gotten sick and been unable to bring charges against Jesus until the next day?

What if they had run out of time for the trial and rescheduled it to Monday?

What if Pilate had listened to his wife and chosen not to issue the death penalty?

What if Joseph of Arimathea had been delayed on his trip to Jerusalem and been unable to take down the body of Christ or place it in the tomb?

The point is this: when our hour comes, an amazing orchestration by God has already set the stage for its fulfillment. God has done all the hard work. We need only to follow through on what we have been asked to do. If we miss that moment for some reason, the Almighty's purposes will still be accomplished. But it will come through another person who is ready.

The ultimate hour for us will be when we finally stand before the Lord. As the followers of Jesus, we have the promise of heaven, but the hour will reveal whether we built on our relationship with Him using gold, silver, and precious stones or wood, hay, and straw (1 Cor. 3:11–15).

Before that epic moment arrives, we will have at least one (if not many more) defining hour for our lives when we are critically poised to fulfill God's purpose in a unique way. The risk is that we will fail the test and the hour will pass us by, the task to be fulfilled by someone else.

Mary and Joseph

Aside from the life of Jesus, probably the greatest example of being ready when the hour came was that of Mary and Joseph. Mary was most likely a teenager and Joseph only a few years older. They already had a deep relationship with the Lord, knew His Word, and lived lives of integrity. Being ready for God's great assignment at so young an age was quite exceptional.

They could not comprehend the magnitude of the events that were poised to take place. Their coming hour was heralded by a personal visit from an angel who did not go into much detail. They responded by faith and accepted what they had been told. The gospel of Luke quotes Mary's response "Behold, the bondslave of the Lord; may it be done to me according to your word" (1:38). The gospel of Matthew shares that Joseph "did as the angel of the Lord commanded him, and took Mary as his wife, but kept her a virgin until she gave birth to a Son; and he called His name Jesus" (1:24–25).

Mary and Joseph's acceptance of God's assignment meant being falsely stigmatized for her pregnancy prior to marriage and the possibility of being stoned to death for it. They faced the danger of being hunted by the megalomaniac Herod, who intended to kill their newborn son, whom he saw as a rival. Barely keeping one step ahead of the pursuit, they escaped to Egypt by night and stayed in exile until Herod died. Even upon returning, they were warned to avoid Herod's malevolent son Archelaus, and they skirted his territory to live in the small village of Nazareth.

Think of the staggering consequences for humanity if they hadn't been ready when their hour arrived.

Joe and Beth

Next to Mary and Joseph, there was another couple in the Scriptures whose story is amazing. As a husband-and-wife team, they rescued the nation of Judah and demonstrated the principles of lives that finished well. In contrast to their famous counterparts, their story is unknown to most of us. What is memorable about this couple is that they receive one of the few finishing-well commendations in the Scriptures.

Who is this couple? Have you ever heard of Jehoiada and Jehoshabeath? Their story is told in 2 Chronicles 22–24. For simplicity's sake, we'll call them Joe and Beth.

Their story begins with the death of the godly king Jehoshaphat in 2 Chronicles 21:1. His son Jehoram assumed the throne of Judah when he was thirty-two years old. Unlike his father, Jehoram chose evil and killed all his brothers as soon as he was in power (2 Chron. 21:4). He wanted no challengers to his rule.

Elijah the prophet later paid him a visit, declaring that Jehoram was under judgment from God for the evil he had done. Unfortunately, his heart remained unchanged. The text says, "The LORD smote him in his bowels with an incurable sickness ... and he died in great pain" (2 Chron. 21:18–19). He grasped for power but had only eight years to wield it (2 Chron. 21:12–20).

Ahaziah, Jehoram's youngest son, became king in his early twenties. His pitiful reign lasted only one year. His treacherous mother, Athaliah (daughter of the evil king Ahab and Jezebel, 2 Kings 8:18), was described this way in the Scriptures: "He [Ahaziah] also walked in the ways of the house of Ahab, for his mother was his counselor to do wickedly" (2 Chron. 22:3). She was a worshipper of Baal and advised her son to pursue evil as his father had. What a pathetic influence from a mother.

Now the plot starts to thicken. Ahaziah was captured in battle and put to death before his reign had hardly begun. His mother, Athaliah, saw her chance to steal the throne for herself. She acted quickly and lethally by destroying all the royal offspring of the house of Judah (2 Chron. 22:10). It was a brazen act that established her as queen and threatened to extinguish the line of David from the throne of Israel.

In the midst of this national crisis, God's big assignment landed front and center for Joe and Beth. It would take all their years of preparation to fulfill the task that was before them.

When Athaliah was in the midst of hunting down all the royal children, Beth moved swiftly and stole away baby Joash, hiding him in a back bedroom with his nurse. She put her life at risk and responded in the moment with great courage. Then, secretly, she moved Joash to the house of God and kept him hidden there for seven years. It took ingenuity and around-the-clock diligence on her part to keep a baby and small child unnoticed for this length of time.

Beth never practiced how to rescue a baby king from death during her previous years of life. But an event took place in her childhood that had planted a seed for something God would use decades later.

Here's what happened. King Jehoram, whom we read about earlier in this story, had a daughter—Beth in this story. As a young girl, she witnessed her father murder his brothers, along with many national leaders, in cold blood. The memory of that despicable act was seared into her mind.

She chose to marry a priest, perhaps indicating disgust with her father and the political world he represented. It set her on a different path. The marriage exposed her to what a life of devotion to God looked like, and she fully embraced it. Over the years, she also gained wisdom in learning how to live in two different worlds—the royal court and the priestly one.

When Athaliah usurped the throne, Beth couldn't allow the slaughter of another member of the royal family without doing something. The seed God had planted in her heart decades before kicked into full force with her rescue of the baby and future king of Judah.

While this was going on, Joe also began working behind the scenes. He quietly put plans into place to overthrow Athaliah that went undetected by her spies.

Here is a surprising fact. Joe was eighty-three years old when his assignment came from the Lord. Beth was probably around eighty years old when she rescued Joash. Their story illustrates that our most significant time of service to the Lord could happen in our later years.

That idea goes against modern thinking. Many believe our main accomplishments occur during younger years at the height of a career well before we hit the eighth decade. Joe and Beth's actions remind us that we need to be ready for God's next assignment no matter how old we are.

Being Ready

It is an added blessing when both a husband and a wife are equally ready to take on a larger assignment from the Lord. If offered a choice, Joe and Beth most likely would not have picked the mission they were given. But they were willing to do what was required of them.

Joe and Beth's task was a long and secret one. Can you imagine what it would have been like to keep their plans to overthrow the government hidden for seven years? Each day held the risk of being discovered, as the paranoid Athaliah had her informers everywhere. Courage defined them as they faced the possibility of death daily.

They must have developed a close circle of friends and trusted allies for no one in the palace to have betrayed Beth for hiding the baby. Friends supported her by keeping the matter quiet from the court's watchful eye.

As Joe was swept to the forefront of an unprecedented national crisis, he immediately began a painstaking planning process to put Joash on the throne and restore the line of David. Because of the secrecy required, it took seven years to accomplish.

His approach to managing this huge task provides an excellent model for any undertaking we might attempt today. Here is what he did:

> He picked men of integrity (2 Chron. 23:1–2, 6). Choosing the right people is foundational to accomplishing any great work.
> He prepared a thorough plan (2 Chron. 23:1). A great plan mobilizes the people to achieve much more than they could do by themselves.
> He inspired the people with a compelling vision that required their personal commitment (2 Chron. 23:3). An inspiring vision helps people see beyond to something greater than themselves.
> He organized the people to do specific tasks (2 Chron. 23:4–6). It is crucial that a vision is broken down into specific tasks for people to do so it can be accomplished.

He prepared for opposition (2 Chron. 23:7–10). Any great undertaking will face detractors who must be dealt with if they arise.

He planned a celebration (2 Chron. 23:11–13). We are remiss if we overlook the benefits of gathering people together to commemorate what has been accomplished.

He demonstrated courage (2 Chron. 23:14–15). When courage is demonstrated, it inspires others to have it as well.

He called everyone to follow the Lord (2 Chron. 23:16–19). When people's faith is strengthened, it makes them ready for God's next assignment.

He persevered until all his goals were achieved (2 Chron. 23:20–21). Persisting to the end is a valuable trait for any undertaking. For Joe, it took seven years to put Joash on the throne. There must have been times when he wanted to quit, but he stuck with it and reaped the reward.

One Assignment after Another

Remarkably, Joe served King Joash for the next forty years and assisted him in every conceivable way. He had leveraged his superb leadership skills to put Joash on the throne and now used them to assist Joash as the new king. Totaled together, Joe dedicated nearly fifty years of his life in the service of this man. Joash benefited significantly from this special relationship. The text says, "Joash did what was right in the sight of the LORD all the days of Jehoiada the priest" (2 Chron. 24:2).

In Joe's case, one big assignment was followed by another. After overthrowing Athaliah, he then had to come alongside the young boy who had just been crowned king. Under Joe's tutelage, Joash grew in the Lord and decided to restore the temple (2 Chron. 24:4). All Israel was summoned to contribute to the repair work, and soon the daily sacrifices began.

Over those forty years, Joe picked two good wives for Joash, seeking to avoid the poor marriage choices made by his father and grandfather. He helped establish political stability so Joash could prosper as king. The affairs of state were guided by Joe's wisdom, and corrupt advisers were kept away. As a result, Joe and Beth were treated as members of the royal family. Their forty-year mentoring role to a king of Judah is a unique story in all of Scripture.

Would we be willing to give our lives to serve someone like this? Joe and Beth's answer was yes as they stepped into a new decades-long assignment from the Lord.

Finishing-Well Statement

In one of its rare occurrences, the Scriptures give a strong finishing-well statement commending Joe's life:

> Now when Jehoiada reached a ripe old age he died; he was one
> hundred and thirty years old at his death. They buried him in
> the city of David among the kings, because he had done well in
> Israel and to God and His house. (2 Chron. 24:15–16)

Joe had reestablished the line of David on the throne, helped rebuild the temple, and restored temple sacrifices, which had encouraged the faith of the Israelites. By giving him the burial of a king, the nation granted the highest honor it could bestow on anyone.

Joe and Beth provide us with one of the best examples in Scripture of a couple who finished well. All five parts of our finishing-well definition (God, spouse, family, fellow man, God's work) were in right relationship when they stepped out of this life and into eternity.

His Finest Hour

Winston Churchill spoke about the significance of being ready in his speech "His Finest Hour":

> To each there comes in their lifetime that special moment
> when they are figuratively tapped on the shoulder and offered
> a chance to do a very special thing, unique to them and fitted
> to their talents. What a tragedy if that moment finds them
> unprepared or unqualified for the work which would be their
> finest hour.[2]

Our goal is to be ready when our defining moment arrives. God will tap us on our shoulders one day and point us to an extraordinary opportunity to experience our finest hour for the kingdom. Mary and Joseph were ready. Jehoiada and Jehoshabeath were ready. We can be too.

Moving Mountains Moment

We are used to getting ready for all sorts of activities, but staying ready is another matter. It involves an ongoing effort similar to having our bags packed, ready to evacuate if we live on the east coast of the United States during hurricane season. To take the risk and try to ride out the storm is a life-threatening gamble. When it comes to our spiritual lives, we are also told to stay in readiness. "Therefore be on the alert, for you do not know which day your Lord is coming" (Matt. 24:42). While it may seem challenging to be ready each day for a potential assignment from heaven, God is right there to help us do so. The Lord can push aside that mountain when we take to heart His promise: "Yet those who wait for the LORD will gain new strength; they will mount up with wings like eagles, they will run and not get tired, they will walk and not become weary" (Isa. 40:31).

13

DRINK THE CUP

Colorado has fifty-four mountains that rise higher than fourteen thousand feet above sea level. They are called "fourteeners," and only a select few mountaineers have climbed them all. Each summit can be reached without ropes and pitons, but they present the climber with harrowing drop-offs, deep crevices, and narrow ledges to traverse.

My friend Tim Jones is a part of that elite group that has conquered each one. It took him eight years to complete the feat because severe weather restricts climbing to the summer months.

His goal was to "bag" all fifty-four prior to reaching his fiftieth birthday. He asked me if I would hike the last peak on his list with him. I had climbed five other fourteeners, and it sounded like a great adventure.

As we discussed our plans, I realized Tim had left one of the hardest mountains for his final climb. It is called El Diente or "the Tooth" in Spanish. Its location in the Lizard Head Wilderness on Kilpacker Trail in southwestern Colorado seemed a bit ominous.

El Diente

We spent the night at the trailhead to get an early start. The climb was a steep eight miles round-trip with nearly a five-thousand-foot elevation gain. Passing through two and a half miles of alpine forest and meadows took us by a beautiful waterfall fed by snowmelt.

The trek became arduous at 11,500 feet, where all the vegetation gave way to rocky talus and boulders. We could hear where icy water flowed under the rocks, but we couldn't see it.

Without an obvious path, we followed little cairns (rocks stacked on top of one another) that marked the general direction. I thought I was in decent shape but was alarmed to discover I had consumed all my water

Waterfall at El Diente Peak (T. Duren Jones Photography, used with permission)

barely halfway up! Fortunately, Tim had a filtered water bottle that I used to drink snow runoff for the rest of the trip.

Several times as the path got steeper, I thought about turning around and calling it quits. Nearly eight hours had passed, and we still hadn't conquered the peak. Exhaustion was starting to take hold, and I knew I had to get to the top soon.

A Daunting Obstacle

I rounded a turn, hoping to view the summit. Instead, I was dismayed to see that the path narrowed to a rocky ledge barely twelve inches wide. It was about thirty feet across with a five-hundred-foot drop-off on the right side. For the first time in my hiking experience, I felt fear. If I were to lose my balance, I could fall to my death. It was not a good situation, especially because I was already exhausted and my legs were spent.

Tim carefully stepped across, one boot in front of the other, arms extended like a tightrope walker. He motioned for me to come over, telling me that I could do it. I sat there for about ten minutes, contemplating the risk and asking God to help me finish the climb. (I'm not sure that was the wisest prayer!)

Then I stood up, took a breath, and walked across that tiny outcrop. I could see the top now, but there was one final obstacle in my way. This time a snow-covered crevasse blocked my path. It was about twenty feet across at a forty-five-degree angle with another drop-off. All I had to do was push my boots into its steep face and work my way to the other side. However, if the snow broke free under my weight, I would have no chance to stop myself from sliding off the edge. Confronted by fear again, I breathed in and dug my boots into the snow.

Finally, I had made it to the summit and reveled in the incredible views. The trail far below looked like a tan thread winding along the mountainside. Dark clouds began gathering with increasing wind so we cut our time short at the top and started back down.

Drop-off at El Diente Peak (author photo)

I recrossed the snowy gap and narrow ledge without further problems. Fourteen hours later as the sun was setting, we arrived back at the truck and headed home.

Tim had reached a milestone few achieve by summiting all fifty-four of the fourteen-thousand-foot peaks in Colorado. El Diente was my sixth fourteener, but I was so exhilarated it felt as though I had climbed many more.

The Meaning of Drinking the Cup

While I had been ready for an adventure on the mountain, it came down to actually doing the hard work of summiting. Many times during the climb I was ready to call it quits, as the difficulty was much harder than I had anticipated. Yet I had committed to hiking all the way up with my friend, so I was determined to keep pressing ahead. It seemed like a metaphor of the biblical concept of "drinking the cup," which is the next and most difficult step on our journey to finish well.

We sense the seriousness of the cup by reading what Jesus said about it: "Father, if You are willing, remove this cup from Me; yet not My will, but Yours be done" (Luke 22:42). It was so severe that Jesus sought a way to avoid it, but none could be found. Everything came down to the moment when He willingly drank that devastating cup and bought salvation for mankind by His death on the cross.

"Drinking the cup" means taking action to honor the commitments you have made to the Lord no matter what the cost. It is a determined mind-set that fulfills a divine assignment even though it comes at great personal sacrifice. It does not hold back or turn away but fully engages what must be done.

Climbing a mountain with its hazards is one thing, but living out this spiritual reality in our daily lives is quite another. If we are serious about following Jesus, we will be asked to drink His cup at some point. By earthly standards, one should avoid it at all costs. Who wants to take on something so agonizing as following Jesus's footsteps to the cross? But heaven beckons us to deeper intimacy with the Father and ardent service to His kingdom.

Luke is the only gospel writer who depicted the extreme physical suffering of Jesus in the garden of Gethsemane with this description: "His sweat became like drops of blood, falling down upon the ground" (Luke 22:44). Drinking that cup, which brought on Himself the divine punishment for our sins, was an incomprehensible sacrifice. The personal agony He experienced is beyond anything we can imagine.

It is significant to realize that the garden of Gethsemane was not a quiet setting filled with trees and shrubs. The name Gethsemane means "a winepress of oils" or, more simply, "an olive press." The location was primarily used to extract oil from olives under the weight of huge stones. Jesus purposely led His disciples to this unique spot on the eve of His crucifixion. By doing this, He was saying, "I am going to be crushed like these olives as I bear the burden for the sins of man. My blood will be poured out like the oil that flows in this place."

The words in 1 Peter 2:21 take on a distinctive meaning in this context. The verse reads, "For you have been called for this purpose, since Christ also suffered for you, leaving you an example for you to follow in His steps." Could following "in His steps" mean that we, too, will be asked to drink a similar cup for God in our lives? I believe it does.

However, it is not only about drinking a cup of suffering. A hidden paradox is also here. The writer of Hebrews captured this idea when he wrote, "fixing our eyes on Jesus, the author and perfecter of faith, who for the joy set before Him endured the cross, despising the shame, and has sat down at the right hand of the throne of God" (12:2).

On the other side of the cross, Jesus knew there would be inexpressible joy in the presence of His Father. He would sit on an infinite throne of glory from which all power in heaven and earth would emanate.

For reasons we cannot fully grasp, this process has a divine order—first comes the cross, then the resurrection. First comes a journey through the valley of the shadow of death, then a dwelling in the house of the Lord forever (Ps. 23:4, 6).

Most people will find this a hard truth to accept. Our sight is limited. It is difficult to peer through heartrending circumstances to glimpse redemption on the other side. The contents of the cup can seem too bitter to drink.

Yet in a real sense, Jesus has already swallowed every drop contained in our cups. He intimately knows the hardship of our situations. "For we do not have a high priest who cannot sympathize with our weaknesses, but One who has been tempted in all things as we are, yet without sin" (Heb. 4:15). With compassionate understanding He drinks the cup along with us.

Dietrich Bonhoeffer

Dietrich Bonhoeffer grew up during the upheaval of post–WWI Germany. Rather than pursing a business career as many young men did at the time, he wanted to be a theologian. His faith in God was heartfelt. He didn't care about seeking fame or fortune. He is probably best known for the book *The Cost of Discipleship*, in which he labeled anything that falls short of full obedience to God's Word as "cheap grace." In his mind, this was grace without discipleship or the cross or obedience to the Lord. The benefits of Christianity were emphasized without counting the costs. Bonhoeffer saw the national church in Germany follow this course, which led it to compromise under the pressure of a fascist culture. Eventually, the church went silent before the Third Reich, turning its back on the plight of the Jewish people.

At age twenty-seven, Bonhoeffer was the first prominent Christian theologian to speak out against the growing mistreatment of the Jews. In April 1933, he wrote an essay titled "The Church and the Jewish Question." Included in this text was the compelling statement "It [the church] must not just bandage the victims under the wheel, but to put a spoke in the wheel itself [to stop it]." He went on to say, "Battles are won, not with weapons, but with God. They are won when the way leads to the cross."[1]

The "spoke in the wheel" became a prophetic statement in his life. In less than five years, Bonhoeffer had contacted a small group of conspirators in connection to their political resistance against Hitler. He later joined them. Within ten years, he was behind bars.

The Gestapo arrested Bonhoeffer in April 1943 and took him to Tegel prison in Berlin. They did not give a reason for the imprisonment. He had recently become engaged to Maria von Wedemeyer. He hoped for a short detention since his antigovernment associations were still unknown. Unfortunately, Tegel was his home for the next eighteen months.

The July 1944 assassination attempt on the führer failed, and Bonhoeffer was eventually implicated as part of the larger plot. Events began to accelerate as all involved in the conspiracy were rounded up and taken into custody.

> Bonhoeffer's eighteen months at Tegel came to an end. He was secretly moved to the Gestapo prison on Prinz-Albrecht-Strasse. Dietrich Bonhoeffer was now in the custody of the state. Bonhoeffer's four months in the Gestapo prison were markedly different from his time at Tegel. The cells were underground. Bonhoeffer's was eight by five feet, and he had no opportunity to see the light of day. There was no prison yard in which to walk, no thrushes to hear sing.[2]

In a letter to his fiancée, Maria, Bonhoeffer wrote:

Stifter once said, "Pain is a holy angel, who shows treasures to men which otherwise remain forever hidden; through him men have become greater than through all the joys of the world." It must be so and I tell this to myself in my present position over and over again—the pain of longing which often can be felt even physically, must be there, and we shall not and need not talk it away. But it needs to be overcome every time and thus there is an even holier angel than the one of pain, that is the one of joy in God.[3]

You can observe the truth of his words in Hebrews 12:2: "Who for the joy set before Him endured the cross." Bonhoeffer was able to peer across and see joy through the cruel conditions of a pit-like cell, knowing that death was soon to come.

In February 1945, just after marking his thirty-ninth birthday, Bonhoeffer was transferred two hundred miles south to Buchenwald Concentration Camp. He spent seven weeks there in another underground cell.

Remarkably, Bonhoeffer was able to endure this supreme test of his faith and physical limits. He still held out hope that he could survive until the war ended, marry Maria, and work to rebuild the German church.

Some believe that Bonhoeffer's death sentence came from Hitler himself. The führer went into a rage after reading secret files that revealed more names of the people involved in the assassination attempt. Orders were given to take Bonhoeffer to Flossenbürg Concentration Camp for execution. He was there only twelve hours before being stripped naked and hanged at dawn on April 9, 1945, two weeks before the Allies' victory.

A fellow prisoner later recalled that as Bonhoeffer went to the scaffold, he drew him briefly aside and said, "This is the end—for me the beginning of life."[4]

Bonhoeffer may not have described the fateful events of his final years as "drinking his cup" for the Lord, but they clearly represented it. He held nothing back from the calling of God on his life. He was not only ready but also willing to drink every drop in the cup that had been given to him. Would we have the same courage to drink a similar cup if called to do so?

Drinking a Difficult Cup

There is a man in the Scriptures who chose to confront a national evil as Bonhoeffer did. The confrontation also required putting his life on the line. In the previous chapter, we looked at the remarkable lives of Jehoiada and Jehoshabeath (or Joe and Beth, 2 Chron. 22–24). They influenced the southern kingdom of Judah to remain devoted to the Lord for over a century. This included saving the life of Joash, the youngest son of King Ahaziah, from the murderous Athaliah, who usurped the throne to make herself queen. They helped purge her from power, establishing Joash as king, and served as his counselors for forty years.

After his death, Jehoiada was given royal honors and the people "buried him in the city of David among the kings, because he had done well in Israel and to God and His house" (2 Chron. 24:16). Jehoiada's son Zechariah must have joined with the large crowd of mourners that day and might have played an active role in the funeral as a priest before the people. We recognize from the passage that he was a man of God who followed in the footsteps of his parents (2 Chron. 24:20).

After the death of his father, Zechariah watched as corrupt advisers stepped in to counsel King Joash. It is shocking to see how quickly they were able to turn the king's heart to abandon the house of the Lord and bring back idol worship:

> But after the death of Jehoiada the officials of Judah came
> and bowed down to the king, and the king listened to
> them. They abandoned the house of the LORD, the God
> of their fathers, and served the Asherim and the idols; so
> wrath came upon Judah and Jerusalem for this their guilt.
> (2 Chron. 24:17–18)

God sent many prophets to warn the king about the dangers of his choices. Each of these individuals was drinking the cup of obedience by speaking boldly ("testified against them," 2 Chron. 24:19) to the king and his inner circle.

Unfortunately, there are no guarantees that we will achieve success or the desired results we want by drinking a cup for the Lord. Our part is to follow through on God's orders and then leave the outcome to Him.

The time line is not clear regarding how long it took King Joash to turn away from the Lord and worship idols. The downward spiral appears to have been rapid enough to hit bottom within a year or two.

It is reasonable to believe that Zechariah was granted regular access to the royal court because of his father's long legacy of service. He would have heard the prophets repeatedly imploring the king to return to the God of Israel. Because of his privileged position, Zechariah may have tried to reach out to the king personally, humbly urging him to remember his former faith and the blessings bestowed on him by heaven.

Sadly, all these efforts were futile. In the face of determined apostasy by King Joash and the officials of Judah, God took decisive action. The verse barely finishes with "They would not listen" (2 Chron. 24:19) when we read next, "Then the Spirit of God came on Zechariah the son of Jehoiada the priest; and he stood above the people and said to them, 'Thus God has said, "Why do you transgress the commandments of the LORD and do not prosper? Because you have forsaken the LORD, He has also forsaken you"'" (v. 20). The entire nation received this final word of judgment. Zechariah drank his cup by being willing to speak the words of God to a rebellious king, his apostate advisers, and a disobedient people. It was done at great personal risk.

In response to what he said, they conspired to kill him. Tragically, King Joash forgot all that God had done for him and the forty-seven years of service performed by Jehoiada and Jehoshabeath. He gave the command to stone Zechariah to death in the courtyard of the temple. It was a brutal way to die, as the rocks would shatter the body a little at a time. His murder was so despicable that Jesus referred to it in His condemnation of the religious leaders for their hypocrisy (Matt. 23:35).[5]

This was the defining moment of Zechariah's life. He did not turn away from the consequences of his obedience to the Lord. He drank his cup fully.

If it were possible to look back over his earlier years, we would have seen him drink many smaller cups of preparation. These minor acts of godly commitment grew larger and laid a foundation on which he would eventually stand to confront the highest political leaders of the land.

As with Zechariah and Dietrich Bonhoeffer, it is highly probable that each of us will have a defining moment when we are asked to drink a demanding cup for the Lord. We should not fear that occasion but be grateful to know that God is steadily preparing us with many cups along the way.

Journey of a Coffee Bean

We live in a coffee culture with thousands of flavor choices, with beans coming from exotic places around the world. For all the coffee we drink, it's surprising how little we know about how it is made. I was intrigued to learn the preparation process the coffee bean goes through and discovered a metaphor that applies to drinking a cup for the Lord. See if you draw the same comparison I did.

The finest coffee is grown between twenty-three degrees north and twenty-three degrees south of the equator in tropical, warm environments. It is called the "bean belt" with flavors varying by the soil, climate, and altitude. However, it doesn't begin as the fragrant bean we're used to drinking.

Coffee starts out hidden within a round fruit. When the outer color turns red, it is picked, dried over several weeks, and then hulled to expose an inner bean.

Coffee beans on a tree (iStockphoto, used with permission)

Roasting comes next and is the most important step in the process. Extreme temperatures up to 473 degrees transform the chemical and physical properties of the beans. Based on the heat applied, a light to dark roast is the result. Grinding the roasted beans is the final step before scalding water is applied.

Looking at this journey from the coffee bean's point of view tells a different story. First, he is removed from the comfort of his tree, stripped of all his protective layers, and dried out. Then he is roasted in fire, which releases antioxidants, oils, acids, and proteins he didn't realize he possessed. This process liberates wonderful flavors that were trapped inside. After the roasting is complete, he is packed up and shipped to a far-off destination.

Upon arrival he is ground up, scalded, and poured out into a cup where his full potential is finally realized. A person savors the aroma and the full flavor that result from the long journey made by that little coffee bean.

Crushing Is Part of the Process

The scripture in Isaiah 53:10–12 says:

> But the LORD was pleased to crush Him, putting Him to grief; if He would render Himself as a guilt offering. As a result of the anguish of His soul ... He will bear their iniquities.... Therefore, I will allot Him a portion with the great, and He will divide the booty with the strong; because He poured out Himself to death, and was numbered with the transgressors.

The experiences of the Suffering Servant described here are forceful—"crush," "grief," "anguish," and "poured out." These are also prophetic verses that speak of Christ's suffering in our behalf. In a sobering way, we also encounter these same things on our paths as we fulfill God's profound purposes in our lives. However, the passage doesn't stop at our suffering. There are magnificent outcomes achieved beyond the suffering. We are healed, our sins are forgiven, and we are now His offspring. The writer to the Hebrews also emphasized the incredible results that awaited Jesus on the other side of the cross—infinite joy and supreme rule on the throne of God.

Ground coffee beans (iStockphoto, used with permission)

From the towering example of the Suffering Servant to the smallest corner of creation, a humble coffee bean, we see these divine principles unfold in striking ways. While knowing that incredible blessings come to those who drink the Lord's cup, there is an important factor to consider: we can choose not to go along with the process.

If the coffee bean had a choice to avoid the roasting cycle, he would do it. Who wants to submit to 473-degree heat that alters your insides?

I wonder how many of us step away from God's roasting, grinding, and brewing stages because the process feels too unbearable to continue. The divine program intended to build the full flavor of our character and integrity is interrupted. When this happens, we retreat to a place of safety and take over the controls.

How do we know that the dire circumstances we are experiencing aren't part of God's larger plan for our lives? It seems counterintuitive to endure pain rather than escape it. But what if we bore the adversity and carried it through to the other side? The Bible says we will receive great rewards if we do.

Jesus was inviting us to join Him on this journey when He said:

> Truly, truly, I say to you, unless a grain of wheat falls into the earth and dies, it remains alone; but if it dies, it bears much fruit. He who loves his life loses it, and he who hates his life in this world will keep it to life eternal. If anyone serves Me, he must follow Me; and where I am, there My servant will be also; if anyone serves Me, the Father will honor him. (John 12:24–26)

God uses each stage of this process to make us more like Christ. As we move forward, the course intensifies (from field to drying, hulling, roasting, grinding, brewing, and pouring out), calling for more courage on our part. The goal is that we reach full flavor to be poured out in our final assignment of finishing well in life.

We can learn important lessons about drinking the cup for the Lord from climbing a fourteen-thousand-foot mountain, hearing the story of a young theologian in a concentration camp, reading about a Jewish priest who put his life on the line for others, awing at the majestic depiction of the Suffering Servant, and evaluating the humble journey of a coffee bean. As we fully yield to God and drink His cup, we are far along the ascent to finishing life well.

Cup of coffee (iStockphoto, used with permission)

Moving Mountains Moment

One of the most daunting mountains to block our way is the high peak that requires our bold or sacrificial action in the name of the Lord. A lifetime of preparation often comes down to a singular decision. Dr. Benjamin Rush, a signer of the Declaration of Independence, described a supreme example of this. He wrote in his diary what it was like in the room that day for the fifty-six men who signed the declaration: "Do you recollect the pensive and awful silence which pervaded the House when we were called up, one after another, to the table of the President of Congress to subscribe to what was believed by many at that time to be our death warrants?" Even though their signatures meant a death sentence by the British, they were willing to take that step and entrust their lives to God. We don't know what our futures will hold, but we can be confident the Almighty is there inviting us to trust Him to move this next mountain. Will we accept His invitation? "The LORD is the one who goes ahead of you; He will be with you. He will not fail you or forsake you. Do not fear or be dismayed" (Deut. 31:8).

FAITHFUL TO THE END

I met Sandra some years ago in the retirement community where my mother lives. She was also a resident and told me about her severe illness that seemed to be causing her life to come to a close. During a time of prayer, the Lord impressed these words on her heart: "I would have welcomed you home with open arms, but, Sandy, there are so many who are not ready. I have work for you to do." She has a gift for sharing her faith with the elderly at various retirement homes.

My aunt Carol was one of the recipients of a visit from Sandra. She was eighty-nine years old and in declining health. Over the years I had spoken to her about Jesus and written her letters explaining the gift of eternal life. For reasons she never made clear, those letters went unanswered.

That all changed in what I believe was a divine appointment when Sandra stopped by to see her. During the conversation, Sandra asked if she could read her Billy Graham's booklet *Steps to Peace with God*. After receiving permission, Sandra read aloud each page and at the end inquired if my aunt wanted to receive Christ as her Savior. She thought for a moment and replied, "Yes." Sandra led her through the prayer of salvation and signed the back of the booklet with "Love to my Sister-in-Christ." Six days later, my aunt slipped into a coma and died.

There is never a moment in our lives when the Lord is not pursuing a relationship with us. He placed Sandra just before eternity's door to make sure people hear about their Savior one last time before they enter. My aunt will be forever grateful she had that conversation at the door.

Being a Finisher

Being faithful to the end is an uncompromising attitude that nothing will deter us from living fully for the Lord until we take our last breaths on earth. Every succeeding year promises greater intimacy with the Father and increasing impact in His kingdom. It often is a season of reward in which we experience the fruit of our labors.

A "finisher" describes someone who is faithful to the end. These people finish what they start. They complete their divine assignments. Every shred of strength they possess is thrown into the endeavor of finishing well for the Lord. The apostle Paul said it this way: "I press on toward the goal for the prize of the upward call of God in Christ Jesus" (Phil. 3:14). The phrase "press on" means to pursue with all speed or aggressively chase like a hunter after a catch. It represents an intense effort to achieve a desired result.

I am constantly on the lookout for finishers. You will recognize them by their deep walks with the Lord and the integrity of their lives. They are influencers and encouragers to everyone they come into contact with.

During an early January breakfast at the Glen Eyrie Retreat Center in Colorado Springs, I sat next to a finisher. I had observed this distinguished-looking man with silver hair make his way into the dining hall. He was in an animated conversation with two other men. After taking a seat next to me, he introduced himself as Denny Repko.

He had been on the staff of the Navigators for more than fifty years. He was still traveling and speaking at over eighty years of age. He had just completed a multiday strategy meeting with four global leaders of their ministry. These mentoring sessions were designed to equip them for expanded roles in their overseas discipleship work.

Following breakfast, I asked Denny if we could talk a bit more. When he heard that my book was about finishing well, he recalled one conversation that had profoundly affected him.

It was back in 1963 when Hubert Mitchell, a veteran missionary and friend of Billy Graham's, was invited to speak to Denny's Bible group. During the talk, he made the statement "I've studied Christian leaders, and not many finish well." That caught Denny's attention as a younger man.

Hubert went on to say there were two requests to ask of God in order to finish well. The first was to "ask God for a great love for His Word." The second was to "ask God for a great love for your wife." Denny recalled, "The Holy Spirit hit me over the head with a two-by-four. I still tremble at the thought of not ending well." Both areas became renewed priorities to Denny from that moment on.

As we continued our conversation, I was impressed to learn that Denny had met with the same group of five men for nearly forty years. He said having their support over this long stretch of time had been crucial to his success in staying on the path to finishing well. They developed into a lifelong group that shared every struggle they were having in their lives with no subject off-limits. They knew that anything less would not provide the honesty needed to stay faithful to the end.

As I reflected later on what we discussed, a number of qualities stood out in Denny's life. Perhaps they can help us have the staying power necessary to be faithful to the end.

A Deep Walk with the Lord

Denny showed me his daily prayer journal with cutouts of prayers, quotes, pictures, and pages of prayer requests that he took with him all the time. He shared his life verse taken from Isaiah 58:10–13 that has guided him over the years:

> And if you give yourself to the hungry and satisfy the desire
> of the afflicted, then your light will rise in darkness and
> your gloom will become like midday. And the Lord will

continually guide you, and satisfy your desire in scorched places, and give strength to your bones; and you will be like a watered garden, and like a spring of water whose waters do not fail. Those from among you will rebuild the ancient ruins; you will raise up the age-old foundations; and you will be called the repairer of the breach, the restorer of the streets in which to dwell.

What a great promise from the Lord. I am going to make that one of my life verses too!

A Nurturing Marriage with Your Spouse

Denny commented that it took a long time to learn how to do this. He said, "I went bedsheet white realizing that I needed to share my whole heart and struggles with my wife. She responded very positively to me when I did, and it caused us to gain much deeper intimacy as a couple. After fifty-nine years, I'd never give that up."

Committed to a Lifelong Accountability Group

Denny has met with the same group of men for nearly forty years. "We connect a couple times a year now that we are spread around the country. No subject is off-limits. In fact, the last time we met, the first question was, 'Have you looked at anything inappropriate in the last six months?' We're all older guys, and yet this is still an area we need to watch out for. It keeps us on track with the Lord."

Trusting the Lord through the Heartbreaks of Life

Some family concerns were weighing on Denny's heart, but he knew God was at work in each of them. He and his wife saw the difficulties that his family members were experiencing. They traveled to spend time with their children and grandchildren to be an encouragement to them.

Great Mental Health and Attitude

Denny was hopeful and optimistic about his life and walk with the Lord. As I listened to him talk, he was quick to poke fun at himself. He was a great storyteller, sharing positive memories of what the Lord had done in his life over the years. His attitude of thankfulness spreads to everyone around him.

Remaining Active in Ministry

Even at eighty-plus years of age, Denny was mentoring global leaders and maintaining a regular speaking schedule to the local church. He said the Lord recently gave him the word *reconnect*, which has motivated him to get back in touch with people from his past ministry. "I'm just trying to follow the thread of the Holy Spirit in what I do."

This is a good checklist to determine our progress in finishing well. How do we match up? Perhaps you could select one to work on for the next month or two.

Antipas in Pergamum

There is another man who was a finisher. His name was Antipas. He is mentioned only once in the Bible, yet what is said about him is hugely significant. In the seven letters written to the churches in Asia Minor (Rev. 2–3), Antipas has the distinction of being the only individual stated by name for his faithfulness in following Christ. His martyrdom was the first in the region. "According to tradition he was slowly roasted to death in a bronze kettle during the reign of Domitian."[1]

Antipas lived in Pergamum (located in what is now northwestern Turkey). At that time, Pergamum was the Roman capital in Asia and the center of emperor worship.[2] The city was situated along an ancient postal route, tying it to the six other towns mentioned by the apostle John in the book of Revelation.

THE BEST IS YET TO BE

Pergamum boasted more temples to the gods than any other metropolitan location. The citizens celebrated thirty weeks of festivals to these various gods and additional festivals for the emperors. Some examples of temple worship include the following:

- Zeus (king of the gods)
- Caesar Augustus and other emperors (addressed as "Lord and God")
- Athena (goddess of truth; she stated, "I am the truth")
- Aesculapius (healer represented by a snake, offered "living waters")
- Dionysus (god of wine and the vine, called "the true vine")
- Demeter (goddess of bread, called "the bread of life")

This vast center of pagan worship was a counterfeit to the truth that Jesus introduced with the gospel. It is fascinating to realize that Jesus responded to every one of the false claims made by these gods through His life and miracles.

It might also explain why Pergamum is described as the place "where Satan's throne is … and where Satan dwells" (Rev. 2:13). It would not have been an easy place to live as a follower of Jesus Christ.

In the midst of this idolatrous culture, Jesus delivers a message to the church in Pergamum and commends the life of Antipas by saying, "I know where you dwell, where Satan's throne is; and you hold fast My name, and did not deny My faith even in the days of Antipas, My witness, My faithful one, who was killed among you, where Satan dwells" (Rev. 2:13).

We learn three things about Antipas:

1. He witnessed for the Lord in this godless city.
2. He followed God faithfully.
3. He died as a martyr for Jesus.

Antipas is an example of someone who was faithful to the end. We don't know how old he was, but nothing deterred him from obeying what the Lord asked him to do.

William Tyndale

Like Antipas, William Tyndale (1494–1536) also held the distinction of finishing well for the Lord at the cost of his life. If you are not familiar with him, he was the first person to print the New Testament in the English language (1525) using Gutenberg's movable-type printing press.

Tyndale's passion was to translate the text of the Bible into the language of the people. This effort brought condemnation from the religious and political authorities who then banned him from England, forcing him to complete his work in Germany and other countries.

He was ultimately betrayed by a man he had befriended named Henry Phillips, who was a guest at many of his meals. Phillips lured Tyndale away from the safety of his quarters and delivered him to imperial authorities under a charge of heresy.

After months of trial, Tyndale was condemned to death and burned at the stake in 1536. His last words were reported to be "Lord! Open the eyes of the King of England." Seventy-five years later, in 1611, scholars worked on the King James Bible and utilized William Tyndale's translation because of its high quality.

Cecilia

It should be noted that being faithful to the end does not relate to how old or young we are, but to our willingness to wholeheartedly fulfill God's calling in our lives. A young woman named Cecilia powerfully illustrated this during her life in the second century in Rome. She was a devout follower of Jesus who lived out her faith publicly. Eventually, her actions came to the attention of the Roman authorities for refusing to worship their gods. They condemned Cecilia to death and tried first to suffocate her by heat in a confined room. When that didn't work, a soldier was dispatched to behead her. The law allowed only three attempts by an executioner, which she survived, but she died several days later from the mortal wounds.

Sculpture of *The Martyrdom of Saint Cecilia* (Bridgeman Art Library, used with permission)

Stefano Maderno, an Italian artist, created a sculpture of her in 1599 called *The Martyrdom of Saint Cecilia*. Under his skilled hand, the marble took on a lifelike appearance. The cuts in her neck are shown, but more significant is the pose of her hands. Her right hand holds out two fingers and the left hand one finger, symbolizing her belief in the Trinity.[3]

When I first saw this sculpture, it moved my heart. Would I have the courage to hold steady in the face of martyrdom as Cecilia did? Could I die with an unwavering belief in the Father, Son, and Holy Spirit symbolized by the gestures of my fingers? If I must pay that ultimate price some day, will I be faithful to the end like all the believers on whose shoulders I stand? These are important questions to ponder as cultures around the world are becoming more hostile to those who follow Jesus.

Sculpture of *The Martyrdom of Saint Cecilia* (Bridgeman Art Library, used with permission)

I pray that we will be inspired by the examples of

Sandra, Denny Repko, Antipas, William Tyndale, and Cecilia, adding our stories of faith and courage to theirs in the great record books of heaven. The crown of righteousness (see 2 Tim. 4:8) will someday be awarded to us as it has been bestowed on those who have gone before. Until that day comes, we have much left to do as we continue being faithful to the end for our almighty God.

Moving Mountains Moment

The longest tennis match in history lasted eleven hours and five minutes. John Isner of the United States and Nicolas Mahut from France were the players. The match took place over three days in 2010 at Wimbledon, England. There were 980 points scored as neither player could break the other's serve. Isner finally won with a simple backhand stroke down the line. It became a worldwide story for the length and intensity of the game. Great feats of athletic prowess are momentary, but exciting, events compared to the lasting adventure of fulfilling God's plans for our lives. As we stay faithful to the end, we continue to see mountains moved as the Almighty uses us in ways we never expected. "For I am confident of this very thing, that He who began a good work in you will perfect it until the day of Christ Jesus" (Phil. 1:6).

PART FOUR

THE CULMINATION

Winning the Battle for Moving Mountains

15

THINK DIFFERENTLY

Joshua was now the leader of Israel. For the second time, he stood at the border of the land God had promised the Israelites. His first visit had been forty years earlier when he scouted out the territory for Moses. He had brought a favorable report about the region and was ready to take possession of it.

Unfortunately, the people were consumed with fear—fear of their enemies, fear of their weaknesses, and fear that God would not help them. They had forgotten the miraculous deliverance from Egypt, the parting of the Red Sea, the pillars of cloud and fire that guided them, the provision of food and water in the wilderness, and God's other supernatural events. They could have enjoyed the blessings of a bountiful land, but instead, their unbelief trapped them in the desert wasteland for four decades.

That fearful generation finally died out, and once again God's promises were for the taking. The Promised Land was wide open before them.

As they were poised to enter, the Lord spoke words of courage into Joshua's heart that would become the hallmark of his life:

> Every place on which the sole of your foot treads, I have given
> it to you, just as I spoke to Moses.… No man will be able to
> stand before you all the days of your life. Just as I have been
> with Moses, I will be with you; I will not fail you or forsake
> you. (Josh. 1:3, 5)

Joshua had been rehearsing this moment for forty years. He was ready, but what about the people?

His first command to the nation as the new leader was unusual: "Consecrate yourselves, for tomorrow the LORD will do wonders among you" (Josh. 3:5). Rather than ordering the people to sharpen their swords and dress for battle, Joshua called them to the most important step of military preparation—full dedication to the Lord. The victories to come were going to be the result of God's intervention, not their own.

The Almighty did not delay in demonstrating His power. The first wonder occurred the next morning at the Jordan River, which was overflowing its banks at the time. When the priests carrying the ark of God stepped into the current, the waters instantly started backing up. The priests remained in the middle of the river, holding the ark of the covenant until all the people crossed over on dry ground. For a second spectacular time, God parted the waters for His people. Thus began the conquest of the Promised Land.

Jericho was the first city to fall by one of the Lord's wonders. He instructed Joshua to march around the city seven times. On the seventh day they were to blow the trumpets with a loud shout from the people. Unbelievably, the walls fell down and the city was taken.

One after the other, the kings of the cities and larger territories fought against Israel's advancing army. Even the dreaded Anakim, who once struck so much fear into the hearts of the people, were defeated (Josh. 11:18–21). Joshua and Caleb proved that God was great enough to deliver their enemies into their hands—the Anakim were no more.

To help his commanders increase their confidence in God's power to give future victories, Joshua provided them with an unforgettable object lesson. Five kings had been captured during one battle and were being held in a cave (Josh. 10:16–27). Joshua gave orders to bring them outside. All Israel's fighting forces were called to watch as these regal men stepped into the sunlight dressed in their royal attire and stately crowns.

What Joshua did next demonstrated his supreme faith in God and brilliance as a leader. He grabbed the kings and threw them to the ground. He invited his commanding officers to put their feet on the necks of the enemy rulers.

As they stood on the throats of the kings they had once feared, Joshua told them, "Don't ever be afraid or discouraged.... Be strong and courageous, for the LORD is going to do this to all of your enemies" (Josh. 10:25 NLT).

From that moment on, the army of Israel swept across the land succeeding in every battle against opposing forces. The text describes the wide range of locations where the battles took place as being in "the hill country, the western foothills, the Jordan Valley, the mountain slopes, the Judean wilderness, and the Negev" (Josh. 12:8 NLT). The diversity of the terrain presented new battlefield challenges for the army. Joshua had to develop unique approaches and tactics to fight in each situation. Although God was going before them, it wasn't an easy path. The infantry pressed forward, triumphing over obstacles that had caused a former generation to flee.

Joshua's skills as a commander and his success on the battlefield were quite notable. But how great of an achievement was it? Do you know how many kings he had to conquer? The end of Joshua 12 records the number—thirty-one! Each one had to be personally confronted and vanquished in hand-to-hand combat.

Often the kings banded together to form larger armies of resistance, hoping to overrun Israel. Even this strategy didn't work. God led the Israelites to victory in each conflict, bringing them closer to the reality of possessing the Promised Land.

Spiritual Battleground

We are also battling enemy kings in our lives today. The apostle Paul used a military metaphor when he wrote about the spiritual conflict being waged:

> For though we walk in the flesh, we do not war according to the flesh, for the weapons of our warfare are not of the flesh, but divinely powerful for the destruction of fortresses. We are destroying speculations and every lofty thing raised up against the knowledge of God, and we are taking every thought captive to the obedience of Christ. (2 Cor. 10:3–5)

Strong military words are chosen to describe what is going on. Walls are being torn down and fortifications demolished. No matter how built-up they might be, barriers are removed and enemies are taken prisoner.

Paul was emphasizing a crucial point in living out our faith. The territory of the mind is where the great battles on earth take place. It is here that Satan places his kings to stand against us and the work of God in our lives. But just like Joshua and the army of Israel, we can overthrow these kings too.

The image of Joshua's commanders standing on the necks of the fallen kings may have been in Paul's mind when he wrote to the Ephesians. In one of the most exceptional texts in all Scripture describing the supreme authority of Christ, we read that He is "far above all rule and authority and power and dominion, and every name that is named, not only in this age but also in the one to come. And He put all things in subjection under His feet" (Eph. 1:21–22). Essentially, these verses are saying that the foot of Jesus is on the neck of Satan, who writhes in submission under its crushing force.

In his book *Spiritual Weapons to Defeat the Enemy*, Rick Renner writes:

> Remember—the most important battlefield of your life is your mind! Spiritual warfare is primarily a matter of the mind. As long as the mind is held in check and is renewed to right thinking by the Word of God, the majority of spiritual attacks will fail. However, when the mind is left open and

unguarded, it becomes the primary battlefield Satan uses to destroy lives. Once you pull the plug on his intimidating threats and lies, he will no longer be able to hold your mind captive. If, however, you do not learn how to take your thoughts captive, your mind and emotions will be used as tools of Satan to dominate your thought processes for the rest of your life.[1]

Paul covered this same theme in his letters when he emphasized the importance of having victory in the way we think. He wrote about it to believers wherever his travels took him. Here are some of his exhortations:

> To believers in Italy: "Do not be conformed to this world, but be transformed by the renewing of your mind" (Rom. 12:2).
> To believers in Greece: "Finally, brethren, whatever is true, whatever is honorable, whatever is right, whatever is pure, whatever is lovely, whatever is of good repute, if there is any excellence and if anything worthy of praise, dwell on these things" (Phil. 4:8).
> To believers in Asia Minor: "Be renewed in the spirit of your mind" (Eph. 4:23).

The Kings We Fight

Let me introduce you to four powerful kings that serve our Enemy and are waging war against our minds at this very moment. They are similar to the Anakim, the giants who lived in the Promised Land and terrified the spies Moses sent (Num. 13:28–33). These kings are trespassers and squatters who will control as much territory in our thinking as we allow them to. Their "fortified cities" are built on the lies, wounds, abuse, and brokenness that took place when we were young. Sadly, we believed most of what they said.

They go by these names:

- King of Rejection—*You are unwanted and excluded.*
- King of Fear—*You are weak and cowardly.*
- King of Failure—*You are defeated and disqualified.*
- King of Low Self-Esteem—*You are worthless and discarded.*

These tyrants spawn many lesser emissaries who further twist the truth. Left unchallenged, they will seek to defeat everything we attempt to accomplish for God. We know the kings have occupied the lands of our minds if we have ever heard them say things to us like the following:

- *You are a loser.*
- *You are ugly.*
- *You are defeated.*
- *You are hopeless.*
- *You are dumb.*
- *You aren't capable.*
- *You don't know anything.*
- *You aren't liked.*
- *You don't deserve it.*
- *You won't make it.*
- *You aren't successful.*
- *You are left out.*

You probably can add many more. If we believe them, these statements can have devastating consequences in our lives. Are there other kings you can identify that are spewing their deceptions? As an exercise, try making a list of what these kings are saying to you. You might be surprised how long it is. By writing it down and acknowledging these kings, you bring the Enemy's lies into the light, where you can confront them with God's truth.

Even as the Israelites continued their triumphant march across the land, watching God give them one victory after another, they still struggled with doubts. The enemy kings continued to intimidate them.

In one case, the sons of Joseph complained to Joshua that the territory they were given was occupied by Canaanites who had "chariots of iron." Granted, chariots were daunting weapons that weren't in their arsenal. But hadn't they recently defeated the Anakim, the huge giants, who had overpowering physical strength? Did the presence of an iron chariot now threaten God's ability to conquer?

It is encouraging to observe that Joshua did not rebuke them for their fear. Rather, he reminded them that they, too, possessed great power and were a numerous people. He inspired them to stretch out to the farthest corners of that region. While acknowledging that the enemy was strong and used the latest iron technology, he rallied them by saying, "Go and drive them out!" And they did just that (see Josh. 17:16–18).

We can probably identify with the plight of the sons of Joseph. Why do we frequently see our weaknesses rather than God's power to deliver? While the Lord of Hosts defeated thirty-one kings in the land, that fact won't help us in the next battle if we don't remember it. Like Joshua's commanding officers, we can stand on the necks of the kings that wage war against us.

Realizing God's Greatness

A friend of mine, Jacki, shared that she was introverted and shy and battled depression well into her twenties. During a time of prayer, she was wrestling with God and told Him, "I am nothing! I have nothing! I am a nobody!" Almost immediately, she heard God's quick answer: "Jacki, I made all the universe out of nothing, so that is not a problem for Me." Hearing that reply created a turnaround in her life and thinking.

Jacki believed what she heard from God and was able to apply His truth to her situation. The kings had been feeding her a lot of lies about herself, but those lies lost their power when she understood who she was in Christ.

The principal way to wage war against the Enemy and his kings is to shine the piercing light of God's truth onto their dark deceit. James wrote, "Submit therefore to God. Resist the devil and he will flee from you" (James 4:7). As we deepen our understanding of God's Word and our authority as believers in Christ, the kings will fall under our feet.

Many followers of Jesus erroneously think that God and Satan are nearly equal in power battling for control of the universe. Satan appears to be winning frequently, and they wonder if God is going to be able to overcome him. Of course, this mind-set is part of an elaborate bluff by the Enemy to deceive us.

If you have any questions about who is in charge, ponder the greatness of God from these verses. It will be evident that no comparison is possible between the almighty One and the evil one. It would be as ridiculous as a grain of sand boasting against Mount Everest or a crack in the sidewalk thinking it was greater than the Grand Canyon.

> Then I saw a great white throne and Him who sat upon it, from whose presence earth and heaven fled away, and no place was found for them. (Rev. 20:11)

> Hallelujah! Salvation and glory and power belong to our God.... Hallelujah! ... Hallelujah! ... Give praise to our God, all you His bond-servants.... Hallelujah! For the Lord our God, the Almighty, reigns. (Rev. 19:1–6)

> [Jesus is] far above all rule and authority and power and dominion, and every name that is named, not only in this age but also in the one to come. And He put all things in subjection under His feet. (Eph. 1:21–22)

Ah Lord GOD! Behold, You have made the heavens and the earth by Your great power and by Your outstretched arm! Nothing is too difficult for You ... O great and mighty God. The LORD of hosts is His name; great in counsel and mighty in deed. (Jer. 32:17–19)

But in all these things we overwhelmingly conquer through Him who loved us. For I am convinced that neither death, nor life, nor angels, nor principalities, nor things present, nor things to come, nor powers, nor height, nor depth, nor any other created thing, will be able to separate us from the love of God, which is in Christ Jesus our Lord. (Rom. 8:37–39)

God is infinitely supreme, unrivaled, and unequaled. How brazen the Enemy is to try to convince us his power is a match for the King of Kings and Lord of Lords.

To take our stand against the evil one, we must deepen our knowledge of God's magnificence and become fully assured of His power. One way to do this is to create a list of all the attributes of God that we can think of. The verses we just read are an excellent place to begin and remind us that there is nothing within ourselves that can overcome the Enemy but God alone.

During a drought in my spiritual life, I felt battered by the Enemy. I knew I lacked a deep understanding of God's characteristics, so I started working on my own list of descriptions. Here is some of what I wrote down:

- Mighty God
- King of Kings
- Lord of Lords
- Most High
- Everlasting Father

- Marvelous Savior
- Prince of Peace
- Wonderful Counselor
- God of Blessings
- Glorious Creator
- God Who Shows Up
- Holy One
- Final Judge
- Lover of My Soul
- Deliverer

This list clearly indicates that God is not fearful, confused, weak, or anything else that we struggle with. Our language doesn't contain the words to fully describe Him. Paul tried to express it by putting together three of the strongest descriptive words possible when he said that God is "able to do far more abundantly beyond all that we ask or think" (Eph. 3:20). We could string a thousand adjectives together, but we still wouldn't come close to capturing His grandeur.

The Psalms are filled with many descriptions that the writers put together to portray God. Let's look at the list King David wrote in Psalm 86:

- God is good (v. 5).
- Ready to forgive (v. 5).
- Abundant in love (v. 5).
- Answers my prayer (v. 7).
- God is great (v. 10).
- Does wondrous deeds (v. 10).
- No God but You (v. 10).
- Delivers me (v. 13).
- Great in love (v. 13).
- Merciful (v. 15).

- Gracious (v. 15).
- Slow to anger (v. 15).
- God of truth (v. 15).
- God of strength (v. 16).
- Helps me (v. 17).
- Comforts me (v. 17).

Our Authority in Christ

In addition to deepening our understanding of God's majesty, we need to know our authority as believers in Jesus Christ. Someone who grasps this idea better than anyone I know is my friend Ron Wilson. He gave me a tutorial over lunch one day. Pulling out his Bible, he turned to the book of Ephesians and asked me to read aloud 1:18–2:7. Then came the pop quiz. His question was "What do these verses say about our relationship with Jesus?" Here's what I observed:

- My eyes need to be opened to Jesus.
- I have hope in His calling on my life.
- I have a glorious inheritance with Him.
- His great power is available to me.
- He rose from the dead in strength and might.
- He is seated at the right hand of God.
- He is infinitely far above all rule, authority, power, and dominion. (Ron explained that these referred to angelic and demonic hierarchies in the unseen world.)
- He is infinitely above every name that is named.
- Everything is in subjection under the feet of Jesus. (Remember Joshua's commanders who stood on the necks of the fallen kings? Satan and every evil demon lie helpless in the dirt, groveling under the feet of Jesus.)

Ron agreed but noted I had missed something. "Where was I seated?" came his inquiry. I looked again and saw that Ephesians 2:6 says:

- I am raised up with Christ.
- I am seated with Him in heavenly places.

I got that right, but the questions kept coming. "When you pray, where do you pray from?" I didn't get his meaning so he stated, "You pray *down* from your place seated with Christ! You are praying *down* with His authority over every situation you encounter. You have victory over the Enemy because of what Christ accomplished." He added, "The invisible reality is more real than the physical reality we live in every day."

When I see Ron now, he will ask me, "What is the invisible reality?"

I respond back, "I am seated in the heavenly places with Christ who is far above all rule, authority, power, dominion … and every name that is named … and all things are in subjection under His feet."

He'll smile and give me a high five.

As Ron helped me understand my authority in Jesus, it revolutionized my thinking. From my place seated with Christ, I have successfully battled the four enemy kings that have plagued my life. Even though that has occurred, I know they will continually look for future opportunities to attack.

Evil One Defeated

We need reminding that the epic battle of good versus evil has already been won by the death and resurrection of Christ. At the second coming and final judgment, Jesus will eradicate all that remains of the enemy— from Satan down to the lowliest demon.

What we see now are the desperate struggles of a defeated foe whose final demise is drawing near. Scripture pulls back the heavenly curtain in Revelation 12 to allow us a glimpse into the conflict that Satan started.

The chapter reveals the evil one foolishly waging war in heaven, having recruited about one-third of the angelic realm to follow him (vv. 3–4). During this battle, he is described by five names: Great Dragon, Serpent of Old, Devil, Satan, and the Accuser of the Brethren.

We soon read that the demonic attackers are vanquished and thrown down to the earth (v. 9). At this point, the text shouts triumphantly, repeating five times that Satan has been thrown down. The words could be written with emphasis—the Enemy of God has been *thrown down, thrown down, thrown down, thrown down,* and *thrown down!* Then a thundering voice announces, "Now the salvation, and the power, and the kingdom of our God and the authority of His Christ have come" (v. 10).

Just as the Dragon was cast down from heaven, the text tells us how God's people can defeat him on the earth. Verse 11 reads, "And they overcame him because of the blood of the Lamb and because of the word of their testimony, and they did not love their life even when faced with death."

The blood of Christ destroyed Satan and destined him to hell. Here is what Christ accomplished for us:

> Satan has been rendered powerless through the death and resurrection of Christ (Heb. 2:14).
>
> We have been delivered from the domain of darkness (Satan's territory) and transferred to the kingdom of His beloved Son (Col. 1:13).
>
> Our certificate of debt (Satan's legal ownership of us because of sin) has been canceled by Christ and nailed to the cross (Col. 2:14).
>
> Christ has disarmed the rulers and authorities (Satan and the demonic world, Col. 2:15).
>
> Christ has triumphed over the evil one, making a public display of His power (seen by all the heavenly hosts, Col. 2:15).

Satan realizes all this and knows he has only a short time left before he is cast into eternal torment. Revelation tells us that the Devil has great wrath and has gone off to wage war against those "who keep the commandments of God and hold to the testimony of Jesus" (Rev. 12:12, 17). That's you and me.

Interestingly, the meaning of one of his names, Devil, also reveals a key strategy he employs in waging war against us. Rick Renner explains this further:

> The name, devil, is taken from the Greek word diabolos and is a compound of the words dia and ballo. The word dia carries the idea of penetration, and the word ballo means to throw something, such as a ball or rock. Literally, the word diabolos describes the repetitive action of hitting something again and again—until finally the wall or membrane is so worn down that it can be completely and thoroughly penetrated. Thus the name devil (diabolos) is not only a proper name for this archenemy of the faith, but it also denotes his mode of operation. The devil is one who strikes repeatedly, again and again, until he finally breaks down a person's mental resistance. Once that person's mental resistance has been breached, the enemy then strikes with all his fury to penetrate and take captive that person's mind and emotions.[2]

Standing Firm

Even though Satan is totally overthrown, we know he repeatedly tries to rob us of our freedom by pulling us back into captivity. It's like an inflated ball held under the water. It pops up in your face if you take your hands off it. Similarly, we must remain vigilant against our Enemy. We can defeat him with the spiritual arsenal at our disposal, which is the truth of God's Word and the authority we have in Christ. The apostle Paul used the example of the Roman soldier to illustrate this.

In Ephesians 6, Paul told the believers they needed to be outfitted like a soldier to successfully fight in the spiritual battle. He instructed them to "put on the full armor of God" not only to hold their ground but also to overcome the Enemy. The strength of the spiritual armor came from knowing the Word of God and counterattacking with that knowledge.

Three times Paul stressed the point that they should "stand firm" against the Devil's attacks. It is important to emphasize that when he told them to stand firm, his image was of the Roman soldier who stood in victory, holding his head high, knowing that the enemy had been defeated. This is the stance of the Christ follower who routs the evil one in a spiritual confrontation.

Paul took another illustration from the Roman army to impress on his readers how massive the victory of Jesus over Satan was. Whenever the Romans conquered an enemy, they didn't quickly set off on their next mission. Rather, they stayed to enjoy an elaborate victory celebration. All the captured soldiers together with their commanding officers and high-ranking officials were stripped of their weapons, bound in chains, and then publicly paraded before the local population. Their crushing defeat was on display for everyone to see. Paul had probably witnessed these types of military spectacles before as a spectator.

That was how Paul described Christ's triumph over Satan in his letter to the Colossians: "He canceled the record of the charges against us and took it away by nailing it to the cross. In this way, he disarmed the spiritual rulers and authorities. He shamed them publicly by his victory over them on the cross" (2:14–15 NLT). The note in the NLT Study Bible adds this explanation for verse 15:

> **He shamed them publicly** (literally *he led [them] in triumphal procession*): The Roman army would celebrate great victory

with a triumphal procession. The victorious Roman general would lead the humiliated captives from his campaign into the conquered city. This image vividly captures the glorious victory that God, through the cross of Christ, has won over all hostile spiritual powers.

The significance of this verse cannot be overstated. Paul gave his readers a glimpse of the victory parade that Jesus led in the heavenly realm following His resurrection. Imagine what that might have looked like—Jesus in brilliant splendor riding at the head of the angelic armies of heaven. These mighty hosts shouting deafening victory cries as they stride behind Him. Multitudes of other spectators burst forth with hallelujahs, knowing their debt of sin has been canceled and eternal life has come.

This colossal tribute to the risen Savior, the mighty God, and the Holy Spirit radiates majesty as, far behind, it parades Satan, who cowers, shattered, silent, and defeated before the Lord of Glory. With him the demonic rulers and dark powers grovel, shielding their baleful eyes from the blinding magnificence on display before them.

Compare this to a previous procession that took place on the earth. The crowds shouted, "Hosanna," to the man who came riding humbly on the back of a young donkey. They did not recognize that the One through whom the entire world was made, the Son of God, deity incarnate, was parading before them. Betrayal and the cross of suffering soon awaited Him. From their infested nest of evil, Satan and his dark forces were gloating prematurely as they looked on, thinking they had the upper hand. How wrong they were.

The first procession paraded humility. The second paraded triumph. The swagger of the Enemy was stomped down quickly, being smashed under the foot of the resurrected Christ.

"Praying Down" in Victory

Knowing the supremacy of Jesus over the Enemy of our souls provides the fortification we need to stand against the Devil's constant attacks. This is necessary because the Serpent will continue his doomed assaults on us until he is cast into the lake of fire at the end of time.

Thus, when a barrage of negative thoughts start pouring into our minds, we know attacks are in progress. The enemy kings continue to test our resolve by detonating these kinds of mental explosives about ourselves:

- *You're rejected.*
- *You're a loser.*
- *You're a failure.*
- *You're not gifted.*

About our relationships:

- *Your marriage is hopeless.*
- *Nothing will ever change.*
- *You have no friends.*
- *You're all alone.*

About our future:

- *You'll live in misery.*
- *You'll have no money.*
- *You'll never find your way.*
- *Just give up.*

By knowing the Word of God and the authority we have in Christ, we can "pray down" from our position with Him in the heavenly places as Paul indicated to the Ephesians. Here is an example of praying down to counterattack the assaults in the previous lists:

Lord, thank You that I have conquered the Enemy in all things through Jesus. He is far above all rule, authority, power, dominion, and every name that is named. All things are in subjection under His feet. I am seated in the heavenly places with Him and have overcome the evil one by the blood of Christ and the word of my testimony. Satan, you are rebuked and thrown down by the mighty power of the cross and the resurrection of Jesus. I utterly reject you from my life. I reject your lies and declare that God's truth will reign in their place. Be gone!

The truth of God's Word demolishes the Enemy's attack; he must flee. We can stand our ground in victory.

What is most important is deploying God's truth by faith into each situation. I recommend saying your prayers out loud since the evil one cannot read your mind. Only God is all-knowing! But Satan can hear our words, and he cowers back when confronted by the authority we have in Christ.

Here is another example of what we can say about our identity in Christ, which the Enemy is constantly trying to undermine:

I am not rejected but chosen and appointed to go and bear fruit (John 15:16). God has chosen me and has plans for my life. I am not a failure because God has said He will accomplish what concerns me (Ps. 138:8). I am honored to be a part of what God is doing, and His purposes will be accomplished in my life. Thank You, Lord, that You are at work in my heart. I will do all I can to be a nurturing husband (or wife) to my spouse and a caring father (or mother) to my children. My marriage is a blessing, and I will not be defeated because God's mighty power will help me in all circumstances.

With practice, these kinds of prayers, spoken in the authority of Christ, can have a dramatic impact in repelling the Enemy. He hopes we believe his lies, but they have no power when exposed to God's truth.

Most of us have accepted a lifetime of lies that the Enemy has planted in our minds. This means we need to retrain our thinking. Once we become aware of how pervasive the falsehoods of the evil one have been, it quickly becomes a conscious process to flip our thoughts over to God's truth. With daily effort our minds can be retrained. In the future, thinking correctly based on how God sees our situations can become nearly automatic.

While the voices of the enemy kings can be shut down, they are trespassers and thieves that will constantly probe for ways to take back the ground they have lost. We must remain vigilant to recognize the schemes of the Devil and stand firm against him and his forces.

Mirror Talk

In addition to praying down with the authority of Christ, there are other things we can do to fortify our faith and resist the Enemy. Another idea is to have a daily "mirror talk."

Mirror talking is essentially looking yourself in the eye and declaring God's truth for your life that day. You are acting as your own spiritual coach. A good coach inspires the players on his team by stating who they are, telling them what they need to know about the game, and giving them a compelling vision for what they can become in the future. Talking to yourself this way may seem a little awkward at first, but the point is to declare the grand truths of God that will define the way you are going to think when you walk out the door.

A good time to do this is in the morning before your day is in full swing. This is also a habit that would greatly benefit your children. Their self-images and worldviews can be changed radically for the better as they declare the powerful words of God over their lives. They need to have their spiritual armor fitted securely as well.

Here are suggestions for the kinds of statements to say to yourself:

- "I am chosen and appointed to go and bear fruit, and that fruit will remain."

- "I am chosen and not rejected."
- "I will settle for nothing less than full victory in my life, marriage, career, and relationships."
- "I take hold of Your promises, Lord, and will walk in them today."
- "I will not be defeated."
- "I will glorify God in my life today."
- "I will finish well in life."

As the renewing of your mind continues, here are further examples of the types of declarations you can make regarding your life. Be creative. Write them down on a note card for reference and memorization:

- "I will not have the glory of God robbed from my life!"
- "I will bless, encourage, and inspire others who are in my life!"
- "I will engage in a relentless pursuit until my very last breath to finish well in life!"
- "In the power of Jesus, I will attack the daunting challenges I face with the intensity of the soldiers who stormed the beaches of Normandy!"
- "I will pursue a deep, personal relationship with the Lord in my daily walk with Him!"
- "I will let my view of God grow and push me far beyond I've ever been before!"

In his book *How Successful People Think*, John Maxwell wrote, "Our thoughts determine our destiny. Our destiny determines our legacy."[3] The subtitle is "Change your thinking, change your life." Do you believe that? I hope you do!

However, let's remember that this is not about drumming up a lot of positive thinking. It's not about techniques or saying formulaic words.

Nor is it our human effort that makes the difference. Rather, it is the work of almighty God in our lives. He alone holds the key to our success and creates the transformation of our minds we so desperately need.

Ready for the Next Assignment

In chapter 12, "Be Ready," I raised a question that convicted me regarding my relationship with the Lord. It was "If God was looking for someone to use on an important assignment for the kingdom, would you be the one He'd choose, given your present attitude, behavior, and choices?" At the time, I had to admit, *No, I wouldn't be the one to pick. I'm not ready.*

My answer would be different now. If asked today, I would say, "Yes, sign me up!" It has been the result of a deepening understanding of who God is and my authority as a believer in Jesus Christ. Most of the territory of my mind that was occupied by the enemy kings has been regained. There still remain pockets of resistance that I am engaging in the power of the Lord. But that is to be expected since the fight will continue as long as we are in these bodies. How would you answer the question? I hope that you will be ready to say yes too!

Winning the battle of the mind can dramatically alter our lives and the legacy we leave to future generations. Thinking differently according to the truth of God's Word is pivotal for anyone who wants to finish well.

Moving Mountains Moment

The Waldo Canyon fire in Colorado Springs was the worst in Colorado's state history. It burned over eighteen thousand acres, cost the lives of two people, and incurred insurance claims of nearly half a billion dollars. The sixty-mile-per-hour winds fanned the flames directly toward the one-hundred-year-old Glen Eyrie castle, home to the Navigators' ministry. Amazingly, the fire skirted the property, which many credited to divine intervention. Yet avoiding the fire was not the only problem they faced. The loss of vegetation set up the conditions for severe flooding in the canyon above that ran through the property. An innovative solution was implemented. At the mouth of the canyon an enormous eighty-foot-wide-by-twenty-one-foot-tall steel-cable fence was installed to hold back boulders, trees, and other debris from being swept downstream. This effectively protected the property from future damage.

Training our minds to believe the truth of God's Word is like putting a steel fence of protection into place. The lies, threats, and trash of the Enemy that sweep down from his dark mountain are stopped in their tracks. We are set free to serve Christ fully. "It was for freedom that Christ set us free; therefore keep standing firm and do not be subject again to a yoke of slavery" (Gal. 5:1).

16

THE FINISH

Pope Clement VII commissioned Michelangelo to paint the large wall behind the altar in the Sistine Chapel. It had been nearly twenty-five years since the artist had completed the majestic ceiling of the chapel with its three hundred figures and famous creation of Adam by the touch of God. Now, in 1536, he commenced the painting of another enormous masterpiece. This time it was to depict the last judgment and the second coming of Christ.

The Last Judgment by Michelangelo in the Sistine Chapel (Bridgeman Art Library, used with permission)

Jesus is the central figure commanding the events taking place. He is muscular and powerful, which was a significant departure from the weaker characterizations of Christ portrayed in the art of the time. The patriarchs, apostles, saints, martyrs, angels, and all the chosen elect surround Him in the sky. The scene is one of momentous action as the final day arrives. Hundreds

The Last Judgment by Michelangelo in the Sistine Chapel (Bridgeman Art Library, used with permission)

of figures are animated as they observe what is taking place. Each face expresses a unique emotion. Probably the most gripping image is the anguished look of a man who realizes his eternal fate will be with the damned in hell.

Michelangelo masterfully captured the essence of what it means to be lost. The painting shows a large, solitary man who is being helplessly dragged down to eternal death by hideous creatures.

"The despair of the damned is embodied in this single titanic man, whose isolation enhances the horror. His legs wrapped by a demon, another pulling on his feet, he plummets toward the abyss of hell below. His face half covered with his hand, his shoulders humped, with his one staring eye he conveys vividly the dawning realization of his fate."[1]

Next to this tragic man, Michelangelo placed angels with long trumpets loudly calling forth the elect. He appeared to be driving home the point that this man foolishly missed being prepared for the most important moment of his life. The piercing sound rings in his ears, repeatedly reminding him that he made a terrible mistake.

The Last Judgment by Michelangelo in the Sistine Chapel (Bridgeman Art Library, used with permission)

Scripture describes the scene like this: "And they will see the Son of Man coming on the clouds of heaven with power and great glory. And he will send out his angels with the mighty blast of a trumpet, and they will gather his chosen ones from all over the world—from the farthest ends of the earth and heaven" (Matt. 24:30–31 NLT).

It is interesting to observe in the picture that there are two angels holding books. One is quite small, which signifies the Book of Life. The other is much larger as it contains the majority of the names who are not destined for heaven. Jesus said, "You can enter God's Kingdom only through the narrow gate. The highway to hell is broad, and its gate is wide for the many who choose that way. But the gateway to life is very narrow and the road is difficult, and only a few ever find it" (Matt. 7:13–14 NLT).

The Book of Life

There is one book in heaven that is supreme above all the others. It is called the Book of Life. Contained in its pages are the names of those who will receive the incomparable gift of eternal life with God and experience the exquisite joy of heaven. Above everything else, our names must be found written here.

What do we know about this book?

The most specific references to the Book of Life were written by the apostle John in the book of Revelation:

> All who are victorious will be clothed in white. I will never erase their names from the Book of Life, but I will announce before my Father and his angels that they are mine. (Rev. 3:5 NLT)

> And all the people who belong to this world worshiped the beast. They are the ones whose names were not written in the Book of Life before the world was made—the Book that belongs to the Lamb who was slaughtered. (Rev. 13:8 NLT)

> I saw the dead, both great and small, standing before God's throne. And the books were opened, including the Book of Life. And the dead were judged according to what they had done, as recorded in the books. (Rev. 20:12 NLT)

> And anyone whose name was not found recorded in the Book of Life was thrown into the lake of fire. (Rev. 20:15 NLT)

These last two references to the Book of Life are the most astonishing. They encapsulate the final judgment of humankind with utter clarity.

We will all stand individually before God's throne where the records of our lives will be read aloud from books cataloged in the library of heaven. It is quite possible that angelic scribes are assigned to write down our every thought, word, and action on earth. These volumes will have our names on them and be opened to reveal the choices we made.

Two categories of books will be opened on that day—the general books and the Book of Life. It will be horribly evident to the person hearing only from the general books that a dreadful fate is about to happen. No amount of pleading for second chances will be possible. With a single sentence, Scripture states the doom at hand: "Anyone whose name is not found recorded in the Book of Life will be thrown into the lake of fire." The colossal magnitude of this fate is beyond our comprehension.

Imagine what it will be like when it's your turn to stand before the mighty throne of God on that final day. Your name is called loudly. You are then escorted out before an immense crowd filled with billions of men, women, and angels who are intently watching the proceedings. There is not a sound to be heard as every eye is focused on you and the Ancient of Days presiding as judge. Jesus, who possesses all authority in heaven and earth, stands at His right hand.

A huge stack of books detailing every aspect of your life is delivered and placed before the almighty One. He looks steadily at you and then surveys the pile of books. Turning to His Son for a moment of conversation, He gazes back at you with a smile. With His powerful arm He sweeps the stacked books aside.

Jesus reaches over and draws out a gloriously adorned book, flashing with jewels and gold-leaf pages. He raises it high above Himself for all to see. Then He opens it and turns to a particular page. He runs a finger down the lines, then stops at a certain place.

What happens next is something you will never forget in all eternity to come. The King of Kings, the Lamb of God, the great Son of the Everlasting Father, the second member of the Holy Trinity, with triumphant voice, announces that your name was found written in the Book of Life. It was entered the day you put your faith in His incredible sacrifice on the cross as payment for your sins. Little did you know at the time how monumental that decision was. Now you watch as He steps down and takes you into His arms, welcoming you into the eternal ecstasy of His kingdom while the myriads cheer in wild applause.

The infinite God then stands to address the audience and declares:

> I will wipe every tear from your eyes, and there will be no more death or sorrow or crying or pain. All these things are gone forever. Look, I am making everything new! It is finished! I am the Alpha and the Omega—the Beginning and the End. To all who are thirsty I will give freely from the springs of the water of life. All who are victorious will inherit all these blessings, and I will be their God, and they will be my children. (see Rev. 21:4–7 NLT)

Dot (".") versus Eternity

The enormous significance of that heavenly moment should grip our minds. Nothing in this world comes close to its weightiness. Still, the events happening now on earth can feel overpowering to us. This often dulls our thinking about heaven.

Our existence on earth has been compared to a little dot (".") in relation to eternity. Here is how Randy Alcorn described it in his book *The Treasure Principle*: "Our present life on earth is the dot. It begins. It ends. It's brief. But from that dot extends a line that goes on forever. That line is eternity which Christians will spend in heaven.… Live for the line, not for the dot."[2]

The Son of God came down to our dot, indicating the tremendous importance heaven places on our earthly lives. It is shocking to realize how much is at stake as we live out our brief existence on this blue planet. It's a striking indication of the value placed on each day we are given. Those twenty-four hours are much more precious than we realize.

In the book *The Butterfly Effect*, Andy Andrews also stressed the significance of living with heaven in our sights:

> There are generations yet unborn whose very lives will be shifted and shaped by the moves you make and the actions you take today. And tomorrow. And the next day. And the next. Every single thing you do matters. You have been created in order that you might make a difference. The very beating of your heart has meaning and purpose. Your actions have value far greater than silver or gold. Your life … and what you do with it today … matters forever.[3]

So, how are we going to live our lives from today on? I say we step out from the sidelines and fully enter the fray. We hold nothing back and quit playing it safe. We stop being consumed with our small ideas and pay attention to God's summoning call. We are 100 percent in. No retreats. No delays.

If you have any doubts about your part in God's grand story on the earth, place yourself in another scene. The armies of heaven led by Jesus, who is riding on a majestic white stallion, are coming toward you. You gape in awe at His approaching presence, having to shield your eyes from His, which are like the sun's piercing fire. The radiant crown resting on His head sends out dazzling blazes of light. Before Him everything falls in prostrate surrender.

You feel insignificant and hope the procession will pass by without taking any notice of you. Unbelievably, it turns your way.

Jesus calls a halt right in front of you, and the vast army comes to a standstill. He looks at you favorably, then motions to someone. Quickly, a beautiful white horse is brought to His side. He hails you as a valiant warrior, and you look around wondering who He is talking to. Your heart swells as He invites you to mount the horse and ride with Him into the next conquest. Before you are hardly seated, He dashes away at a full gallop, leaving you and the hosts of heaven racing to catch up.

Over His shoulder He joyfully shouts your name, adding, "Come ride with Me! Ride with Me!" The flying mane of your horse reflects your decision. You have been chosen to ride with the King of Kings to accomplish great ventures for the kingdom.

Three Defining Words

The heart of a life that finishes well can be summed up in three defining words—*integrity, courage,* and *reward.* Grasping their significance is like adding steel reinforcement to a building. Each of them has a unique meaning in the context of this worthy pursuit:

> *Integrity*—Honoring my vows to the Lord and to others for life
>
> *Courage*—Resolving to do whatever it takes to live with integrity
>
> *Reward*—Experiencing the benefits that come from living with integrity and courage

Integrity

Integrity is built over a lifetime. It is a determined commitment to trust God and His Word no matter what the personal consequences may be. In the midst of the storm, it stays the course and does not seek the easy way out.

Living a life of integrity is highly regarded by God. King David and King Solomon saw huge benefits for an individual characterized by it. Here is what they said in the Scriptures about this outstanding quality:

> Let integrity and uprightness preserve me, for I wait for You.
> (Ps. 25:21)

I have walked in my integrity. And I have trusted in the LORD without wavering. (Ps. 26:1)

But as for me, I shall walk in my integrity. (Ps. 26:11)

He who walks in integrity walks securely, but he who perverts his ways will be found out. (Prov. 10:9)

The integrity of the upright will guide them. (Prov. 11:3)

A righteous man who walks in his integrity—how blessed are his sons after him. (Prov. 20:7)

Who comes to mind when you think of someone who demonstrates this kind of deep-seated integrity? Perhaps someone would think of you!

Courage

Courage is bravery in action, safeguarding the integrity of one's life. It stands firm in the face of compromise, corruption, and excuses. No matter how difficult a situation may be, courage pays the price and takes the risk to steadfastly maintain integrity's high calling.

As followers of Jesus in a hostile environment, we need to have a sense of watchfulness and even wariness about the traps all around us because the risks of failure are great. The landscape is strewn with people who have allowed integrity to slip from their grasps. Solomon advised, "Watch over your heart [integrity] with all diligence, for from it flow the springs of life" (Prov. 4:23).

We should note that we are not demonstrating courage for its own sake. We act courageously because there is always an object in sight that is worth striving for. Wisdom informs it so that courage is skillful, accomplished, and certain of its goal. Those lacking this quality are foolhardy and unprepared for the onslaught that inevitably comes against anyone trying to live with integrity. The quote "He fought bravely but died quickly" characterizes these people. They were of fleeting value in the conflict when they could have helped win the battle.

Reward

Throughout the Scriptures, the idea of receiving a reward is a consistent theme. Over twenty-five words are used to express its many meanings. While there is some mystery about what the rewards will be, we know that God "is a rewarder of those who seek Him" (Heb. 11:6). The ultimate reward is the relationship and intimacy we will have with Him in heaven for all eternity. Nothing is better than that! Yet God's generosity is so lavish that He indicates there will be special rewards included as well.

Consider these verses that describe the idea of reward:

> Rejoice and be glad, for your reward in heaven is great; for in the same way they persecuted the prophets who were before you. (Matt. 5:12)

> And whoever in the name of a disciple gives to one of these little ones even a cup of cold water to drink, truly I say to you, he shall not lose his reward. (Matt. 10:42)

> Now he who plants and he who waters are one; but each will receive his own reward according to his own labor.... Now if any man builds on the foundation with gold, silver, precious stones, wood, hay, straw, each man's work will become evident; for the day will show it because it is to be revealed with fire, and the fire itself will test the quality of each man's work. If any man's work which he has built on it remains, he will receive a reward. (1 Cor. 3:8, 12–14)

> Whatever you do, do your work heartily, as for the Lord rather than for men, knowing that from the Lord you will

receive the reward of the inheritance. It is the Lord Christ whom you serve. (Col. 3:23–24)

While these texts puts the emphasis on the rewards that we will receive in heaven, there are still benefits from following the Lord that accrue for us on earth. God sent a prophet to King Asa of Judah, calling him back to single-minded devotion to the Almighty with the promise of reward: "But you, be strong and do not lose courage, for there is reward for your work" (2 Chron. 15:7). Jeremiah repeated this same message to Israel hundreds of years later: "'For your work will be rewarded,' declares the LORD.... 'There is hope for your future'" (Jer. 31:16–17). A life lived before the Lord with integrity and courage will experience rewards both on earth and in heaven.

Queen Esther

Someone who demonstrated integrity, courage, and reward was Queen Esther. She was born in the foreign city of Susa (now in modern-day Iran), exiled far from her homeland of Israel. Both her parents died young, leaving Esther an orphan to be raised by a cousin named Mordecai.

People like Esther, of low societal status, had limited prospects for upward advancement. She couldn't imagine that a single decision made in the palace of King Ahasuerus would forever alter her future. Yet when Queen Vashti publicly dishonored the king during an international banquet, unprecedented events began to unfold. The queen was stripped of her royal title, and a search began across the empire to find a more worthy replacement.

Remarkably, out of all the eligible women in Persia, Esther was chosen to become the new queen. As the imperial crown was placed on her head, she was catapulted from obscurity to prominence. But more important than the earthly coronation was the greater orchestration of the divine plan.

During her early years as queen, Esther exemplified a woman with exceptional personal qualities. From her story, we observe these attributes:

- Listened to the wisdom of elders
- Behaved wisely in her actions
- Endeared herself to those in authority
- Built friendships with others
- Handled herself favorably in public

In addition to all this, she was blessed with physical beauty that complemented the rest of her traits.

Esther had been queen for five years when Haman's plot to destroy the Jewish people became known. When Mordecai found out about the conspiracy, he sent word pleading for Esther to try to avert the genocide. She quickly responded that it meant instant death, even for the queen, to approach the king unannounced. The only exception was if the golden scepter was extended in her direction.

When Mordecai intervened for the people of Israel, he knew the mortal danger of going unsummoned before the king. He was asking the woman he loved as his own daughter to put her life on the line for a supreme need.

What he said next is profound and instructs us about the advancement of God's purposes in the world. While the Almighty lifts up individuals to carry out His sovereign plans, there are others He can call on who will complete the task if we fail to do so. Here is what the Scripture records: "Then Mordecai told them to reply to Esther, 'Do not imagine that you in the king's palace can escape any more than all the Jews. For if you remain silent at this time, relief and deliverance will arise for the Jews from another place and you and your father's house will perish. And who knows whether you have not attained royalty for such a time as this?'" (Esther 4:13–14).

Esther faced the greatest decision of her life. She knew the cost, thought it through carefully, then chose to act—with integrity and courage. Her final word to Mordecai was "If I perish, I perish." There were no guarantees of a happy ending, only the clear path of obedience. Once the choice was made, she laid out a plan of action that included a three-day fast from food and water. Following this, she would make her unannounced appearance before the king.

When she arrived at the throne room, the golden scepter was extended. The king could tell she was troubled, and he inquired about it. Her strategy for delivering the Jews began with a simple request—for the king and Haman to attend a banquet. That first banquet led to a second. With impeccable timing on the final evening, Esther pleaded for her life and the lives of her people, accusing Haman of his extermination plot.

The king was appalled at what he heard. Haman knew that the circumstances had turned against him. He begged for his life before Esther but without success.

Events moved swiftly forward. Haman was put to death, and another edict was issued. This time the Jewish people were authorized to defend themselves in light of the coming attack. They routed their enemies. Seeing the wisdom demonstrated by Mordecai, the king promoted him to second in command over the empire.

While this story had a happy ending, it should be noted that Esther had no guarantees that she would be successful. She could easily have perished given the complexity of events combined with the whims of a despotic king. If that had happened, God would have brought about another way to deliver His people.

Esther's life displayed integrity and courage under the most extreme conditions. But what about the reward?

On a national level, the Jewish people were delivered from destruction. Their enemies fell before them in defeat, and a lasting peace was established. Personally, Esther experienced the joy of knowing that God used her to save the nation of Israel. And she saw her adopted father, Mordecai, promoted by the king to help lead the empire.

Esther's story shows all three defining words of finishing well in action. There's no limit to the ways they can be displayed through our lives. We can be confident that living with integrity and courage will eventually lead us to a season of reward. That could be realized by:

- Seeing our children and grandchildren walk with God
- Serving in ministry far into our senior years
- Experiencing contentment and peace
- Healing broken relationships
- Observing answers to prayer
- Hearing God's voice
- Delighting in close friendships
- Mentoring others who respond to our guidance

People described by these three qualities will be highly esteemed in heaven, forces for good on the earth, and deadly foes to the kingdom of darkness. The impact of their lives will be immense, not only for those living in the present day, but also for future generations. They are like a rushing river carrying their posterity along the channel of God's blessing.

Painting of the Four Horsemen

Like Esther, Mordecai, and the faithful ones who have preceded us, the time has arrived for the story of our life to be told. So many people will be affected by the sentences, paragraphs, and chapters we write. Eventually, our book will be finished for others to read.

In searching back over that, we will have no regrets for having lived a life of integrity for the Lord. That rare quality will have been worth the high price we paid and the courage it required.

In 1987, four men perished in a plane crash as they returned home from a Focus on the Family board meeting. On that flight was businessman Hugo W. Schoellkopf III, forty-three; ministry leader Rev. V. Creath Davis, forty-seven; bank executive George L. Clark, forty-nine; and surgeon Dr. Trevor E. Mabery, fifty-one. When they boarded Hugo's twin-engine Cessna, no one knew it was going to be their last trip on earth.

Of One Spirit by G. Harvey (used with permission)

G. Harvey, renowned painter of the American West, honored the memory of these men in 1988 with a painting called *Of One Spirit*. For many, it became known as *The Four Horsemen*. This piece of art beautifully depicts our journey to finish well, which they exemplified.

As you look at the picture, what story does it tell you?

I imagine that these four veteran cowboys have been friends for years. They've punched cattle, done every job imaginable on a ranch, and slept under the stars more nights than they can remember. A few times they had to stand side by side confronting lawbreakers who came to take what wasn't theirs. They've had their share of injuries, disappointments, and loss, but somehow feeling a steady arm around the shoulder pulled them through the hardships.

Nearing the end of this long trail, it seems that all creation is putting on her best show with the bright yellows and burnt oranges of a glorious autumn. There's a crispness in the air foretelling the changing of the seasons. The sun is starting its descent behind the mountains, splashing color off the surface of the moving water.

As the horses enter the flow, one of the cowboys looks over to his friends and says what they were all thinking, "We're almost home. This is the last river to cross before we're there."

At some point, that will be true for us. We will cross the final river and conclude our ride in this life. Then we will enter through the glorious gates to enjoy the unimaginable ecstasy of heaven.

The Wonder of Heaven

The apostle Paul was close to that moment when he shared the final words of his life in his second letter to Timothy. He beautifully expressed the heart of what it meant to finish well to his beloved protégé. You would not know Paul was writing from a dismal prison cell in Rome, chained up and awaiting death by order of Emperor Nero. According to tradition, he was beheaded on the Ostian Way to the west of the city[4] not long after writing these words:

> I have fought the good fight, I have finished the course, I have
> kept the faith; in the future there is laid up for me the crown
> of righteousness, which the Lord, the righteous Judge, will
> award to me on that day; and not only to me, but also to all
> who have loved His appearing. (2 Tim. 4:7–8)

This was the only time Paul used the phrase "to all who have loved His appearing" in his writings. It held special significance. The way he wrote it could mean both a look to the past at the first appearance of Jesus as well as a look to the future for His triumphant return. The New International Version translates it "to all who have longed for his appearing," which has this latter meaning in mind.

With only days left to live, Paul was reflecting back over his life with the consummate knowledge that he had completed his earthly assignment. Soon his deepest longings would be realized in the embrace of Jesus in heaven.

It was all the more intense because he had been given a glimpse into heaven and knew what was coming. What he experienced was so magnificent it overwhelmed him. All Paul could say about it was that he "heard inexpressible words, which a man is not permitted to speak" and saw "the surpassing greatness of the revelations" (2 Cor. 12:4, 7). He couldn't wait to return there again. But this time it would be called home.

There will come a day for each of us when our heart beats one last time, when our final breath is taken, and we are instantly transported into the presence of almighty God. How wonderful it will be to present Him with a life that finished well and to hear those incredible words, "Well done, good and faithful servant!"

Nothing can compare to that ending to our story. The earthly chapters will have been completed. The heavenly ones will only just be starting.

Moving Mountains Moment

It has been said that we stand on the shoulders of the great saints who have gone before us. If they hadn't passed their faith on to the next generation, we wouldn't be here. May our children, grandchildren, even great-grandchildren say the same about us! It will have been worth every sacrifice and every mountain God moved out of the way to help us finish well. An interesting exercise would be to make a list of the mountains you are praying the Lord will move and see what He does about them in the future. "There is none like the God of [Israel], who rides the heavens to your help, and through the skies in His majesty. The eternal God is a dwelling place, and underneath are the everlasting arms" (Deut. 33:26–27).

PART FIVE

THE COURSE

Charting the Path Forward with Discussion

Questions and Bible Study

DISCUSSION QUESTIONS AND BIBLE STUDY

Chapter 1: Life in Review

Discussion Questions

1. What mistakes have men and women made over the centuries in the pursuit of success that affected their relationship with God?

2. Did any part of Mark Twain's or Mother Teresa's description of life stand out to you (pp. 24–26)? Do they represent any mountains you are facing? Explain.

3. Project yourself into the future and think about your funeral service. What comments from your children or family would you hope to hear about your life on earth? How are you instilling those qualities into your relationships today?

Bible Study

1. Read Psalm 90:10–12. How do verses 10 and 12 relate to why Moses said we needed to be taught to number our days? What does that accomplish?

Describe some personal qualities that would contribute to presenting a heart of wisdom to God.

In what areas are you presenting to God a heart of wisdom? Is there anything that you could improve? If so, aside from praying about it, what could you do this week to start working on it?

2. In Psalm 39:4–7, we read what King David thought about the years of his life.

Write down how he described mankind's life and efforts in verses 4–6.

What did David conclude as the answer to his fleeting life (v. 7)? How does this attitude help as we face our mountains?

3. Are you experiencing God as the hope of your life? Why or why not?

Chapter 2: The Narrow Way
Discussion Questions

1. Write down your personal definition of a life that finishes well. Discuss.

How closely does the definition of finishing well presented in this chapter (p. 45) align with your own? In what ways is it the same or different?

2. As an estimate, what percentage of your family and friends finished their lives in right relationship to *all* five areas (God, spouse, family, fellow man, and work) according to the definition given. What conclusions do you draw from that number? How does that affect you?

3. Was there someone you knew who finished with all five areas of the finishing-well definition? Describe who it was and the qualities you most admired in him or her.

4. Is there one part of the finishing-well definition that feels like a large mountain needing God's help to move? Relying on His strength, what could you start doing this week to work on it?

5. How would you describe your relationship with God at this time? (If you need more information about what it means to have a personal relationship with God, please refer to appendix A.)

Bible Study

1. Read (and memorize, if possible) the following verses that contain the two great commandments of Jesus, and answer the following questions:

> "You shall love the Lord your God with all your heart, and with all your soul, and with all your mind." This is the great and foremost commandment. The second is like it, "You shall love your neighbor as yourself." On these two commandments depend the whole Law and the Prophets. (Matt. 22:37–40)

What type of commitment to God is Jesus after in our lives?

What are some practical ways you could love God with your heart, soul, and mind this week?

2. Why did Jesus rank loving our neighbors as second in importance? What does this tell us about ourselves in relation to other people?

3. In Luke's account (Luke 10:25–37), Jesus told the parable of the Good Samaritan to illustrate what a genuine neighbor does. Read these verses and put yourself in the story. How willing would you have been to get involved with a man stripped, beaten, and left half-dead as the Samaritan did? Explain.

Is there anyone who comes to mind to whom you could be a better neighbor? What might you do to show that person you care?

Chapter 3: High Risk
Discussion Questions

1. Are you experiencing any of the mountains of midlife highlighted in the chapter (deep regrets, crises of faith, marriage problems, financial difficulties, health issues, unemployment pressure, aging parent demands, or adult children struggles)? Which are the most pressing, and where could you use some help in coping with them?

2. The Battle of Normandy was presented as a metaphor for the battle many are facing to hold their marriages, families, and personal integrity together. Do you agree or disagree with this comparison? Is there another metaphor you would use? If so, explain.

Which of the three areas (marriage, family, and personal integrity), or possibly another one, represent the center of the battle for you? Explain your choice.

3. Read the revised Churchill speech on page 55–56. Which part stands out to you?

If you could speak in front of your church or group, what words of exhortation would you say about the need to keep their marriages, families, and personal integrity intact?

Bible Study

1. This chapter had the following quote: "There are 2,930 people mentioned in the Bible and we only know significant details for about 100 of them. Of this group only 1/3 appear to have finished well with most failing in the second half of life." Included in this latter group was King Solomon, the wisest man in the world.

From the following verses, note what characterized Solomon's relationship to God during the first half of his life:

> 2 Chronicles 1:6
>
> 2 Chronicles 1:7–10
>
> 2 Chronicles 6:14–15, 19
>
> 2 Chronicles 6:31

2. What happened to King Solomon in the second half of his life? From the following verses, write down the areas that caused him to stumble, breaking his relationship with God.

> 1 Kings 11:1–4
>
> 1 Kings 11:5–8
>
> 1 Kings 11:9–11

3. What can we do to protect ourselves from the choices that Solomon made that resulted in his failures and broken relationship with God?

Chapter 4: Going Deeper
Discussion Questions

1. How would you describe your relationship with Jesus Christ?

2. If you were to die today and God asked you, "Why should I let you into heaven?" what would you say? If you are unsure, refer to the God's Heart toward Us section in this chapter, or talk with a trusted friend who is a follower of Jesus Christ.

3. Have you been relating to God on your own terms? If yes, what needs to change so you start living according to His terms?

4. What caring descriptions about you from God in Isaiah 43:1–4 mean the most at this time? Are there any you have trouble believing?

5. Did the poem "Maker of the Universe" (p. 67) give you further insight into God's love? If so, describe what you learned.

6. What do you need to do in order to go deeper with God in your life?

Bible Study

1. In Psalm 73, Asaph took an honest look at life. He saw the inequities and injustices that nearly caused him to stumble in his faith in God. Some of the words he used indicate his attitude: "My steps had almost slipped" (v. 2), "It was troublesome in my sight" (v. 16), and "My heart was embittered" (v. 21). Life wasn't working out according to his way of thinking. He had to change his perspective and see things differently on God's terms. Read the following verses, and identify how Asaph came to accept God's view of life.

> Verse 23
> Verse 24
> Verse 25
> Verses 26–28

2. The writer of Hebrews wanted his readers to grow more deeply in their walks with Jesus. From the following verses, what suggestions did he have for them?

Hebrews 12:1

Hebrews 12:2

Hebrews 12:3

3. Isaiah 43:1–4 communicates God's heart toward us. Read this passage aloud, speaking your name in verse 1 where it says "Jacob" or "Israel."

Can you apply any of these verses to the mountains you are facing now? If so, write down your thoughts.

Write a prayer of thanks to God (or pray aloud) for what He has promised to do in your life. Be sure to combine your needs with His promises.

Chapter 5: Mr. and Mrs.

Discussion Questions

1. Do you know anyone who has experienced a strong marriage? Describe the qualities that helped them enjoy a good relationship.

2. For a marriage that did not last, what do you think were some reasons it failed?

Do you think the marriage could have been rescued? Why or why not?

3. If you are married, what is one thing you appreciate about your spouse?

4. In this next week, what could you do to model God's love to your spouse?

Bible Study

1. God's heart for His bride, Israel, is shared in the profound marriage story located in Ezekiel 16. Read the following verses, and describe the kind of husband He was to her.

> Verse 6: What word did God speak over Israel? What does it mean? How does that word *live* apply to the kind of relationship we want to have with our spouses?

Verse 8: To "spread a skirt over someone" was a symbol of marriage. What points were made regarding God's commitment to His marriage?

Verses 9–14: From the list presented, what stands out to you about God's love for His wife, Israel? Explain.

2. Sadly, Israel was an unfaithful wife to her husband. From the following verses, identify the choices she made that broke the relationship with her heavenly spouse.

Verse 15: Describe where Israel went wrong. How can we protect ourselves from these temptations?

Verses 22 and 43: What did Israel neglect to do? How could she have avoided stumbling into these temptations? How does Revelation 2:4–5 relate to this?

3. After terrible rejection and neglect from His bride, God still pursued her and honored His marriage vow described near the end of Ezekiel 16.

Verses 60 and 62: Why did God seek to honor His marriage vow when He had every right to divorce her?

Verses 61 and 63: When one spouse chooses to honor his or her marriage vow and extend forgiveness, what often happens to the other spouse?

The chapter makes this closing statement about Ezekiel 16 on page 82: "I don't believe this text is saying we must always stay with an adulterous spouse or remain in an abusive relationship. Rather, could it be an attempt by God to radically alter our thinking about the brokenness and dysfunction we find in our spouses and marriage relationships? Could it be possible that we have more room in our hearts to extend forgiveness than we previously thought?" If you're in a situation like this, what do you think God is asking you to do?

4. Woven throughout the book of Hosea is God's love for His unfaithful wife, Israel. He grieves over the loss of relationship with her. He pursues her, forgives her, and restores her. God wanted to demonstrate this love through the example of a husband and a wife, and He picked Hosea and Gomer for the assignment.

Read Hosea 1:2–3. What did God ask Hosea to do? What might have been going on in Hosea's mind? Think about this from Gomer's side. How do you think she was feeling about this situation?

Has God ever asked you to do something difficult in your marriage? How did you react? What was the result?

5. God wanted Hosea's marriage with Gomer to be a living parable (a story illustrating a spiritual truth) of God's love for His people. Could God be making a similar request of your marriage? If so, what do you think the request might involve?

6. Read Hosea 3:1–3. We're not told why, but Gomer left Hosea and her children and became enslaved to another man. What was God asking Hosea to do again? Why was this important?

What do we learn about God's love from Hosea's actions and his heart toward Gomer? Is there anything in this story that might apply to your marriage?

Chapter 6: Pebble or Boulder
Discussion Questions

1. Is there anyone among your family or friends who left a legacy that influenced your life? If so, who was the person and what did he or she impart to you? Note: it can be positive or negative.

Did this person's legacy influence more than one generation? If so, in what ways did that occur?

2. What would you like your children, grandchildren, and great-grandchildren to remember about you?

How can you begin to impart that now?

3. When was the last time you expressed your love or gave caring counsel (verbally or in writing) to your spouse or children? We read that Jacob waited until he was on the verge of death (Gen. 49:33) before he communicated his heart to his sons. What could you do in the next thirty days to communicate your heart to those closest to you? Write down their names and note the completion date.

Is there an event coming up for someone—birthday, anniversary, recognition milestone—during which you could impart your blessing and counsel?

4. If you have a broken relationship with an older child or family member, how could you take a step of action toward restoration? When might you be able to connect with that person?

5. Two analogies were presented that describe the characteristics of the Devil—killer whales working in unison to separate a gray whale mother from her calf and a prowling lion seeking someone to devour. Discuss the characteristics of these predators and how we can defend against similar spiritual attacks in our families and personal lives.

Bible Study

1. Jacob called his twelve sons together and blessed them as recorded in Genesis 49. Centuries later, Moses did the same thing to their descendants who had now grown into great tribes ready to enter the Promised Land (Deut. 33).

> What were the highlights of Joseph's blessing from his father
> in Genesis 49:22–26?
> What did Moses say about Joseph in Deuteronomy 33:13–17?

Could you use anything from this blessings by Jacob in what you might say to your son, your daughter, or another individual?

2. Read 1 Peter 5:8–9. Are we prepared to face our Enemy described as a "roaring lion, seeking someone to devour"? If not, what changes could we make to be ready?

In light of these verses, how can we strengthen the faith of our spouses and children to defend against potential attacks?

3. Abraham left his home in Haran for the land that God had promised to give him. Read Genesis 12:4–7. Note his age, attitude, and actions taken on this trip.

In verse 7, what was God's promise to Abraham?

4. The Bible gives one of its few finishing-well commendations to Abraham. Read Genesis 25:7–8, and note the key points mentioned in the text.

Compare Genesis 12:4 to Genesis 25:7. How many years did Abraham sojourn after leaving his home in Haran at the command of God? It is striking to note that he did not fully possess the land that God had promised to give him. What does this teach us about God's timing and the fulfillment of His promises in our lives?

Are there any expectations you have of God that you want to adjust in light of Abraham's example?

5. The planting of a tamarisk tree is a bold action with a vision to future generations. Someone who planted one would not enjoy its shade. Their grandchildren and great-grandchildren would be the beneficiaries. Read Genesis 21:33–34. How was Abraham's faith shown in what was described in this passage?

Bible historian and teacher Ray Vander Laan asks these questions of his students: "Did you plant a tamarisk tree today? Did you do anything today that will outlive yourself and bless others for years, decades, and centuries down the road?" What do you think about your life having an influence for this long of a time?

Make a list of what you could do that would outlive yourself and bless future generations of your family.

Chapter 7: Unexpected Friends

Discussion Questions

1. Changing the way we view people outside of our social or economic circles can open up doors of influence to their lives. Has your view of anyone changed after you got to know him or her? Explain.

2. Has anyone ever reached out to you to share his or her faith in Jesus or show His love?

3. What attempts, if any, have you made to try to represent Jesus to those outside your normal circle of contacts? Describe.

4. To whom could you be the hands and feet of Jesus?

What might God be asking you to do for them?

Bible Study

1. What are some of the things Jesus did for the people He met as described in the following verses? How might we do similar things for others?

> Mark 8:1–9
> Mark 10:13–16
> Luke 5:30–32
> Luke 12:6–7

2. As the early church grew, great numbers of new believers in Jesus were added to their midst daily. From Acts 2:44–47, what were some of the actions they took that contributed to this?

What similar activities could we do to represent Jesus to the world?

3. Read James 1:27. What does this verse say is "pure and undefiled religion"?

Is there anyone around you who has a need you could meet? If so, what step of faith can you take?

Chapter 8: Assignments
Discussion Questions

1. How would you describe your current assignment(s) from the Lord? Don't worry if you aren't sure what your assignments are. Have you noticed God at work in a particular situation recently?

2. Is there anything that is holding you back from fulfilling God's assignments in your life? What can you do to move forward?

3. What does David Brown's story communicate about the direction God's assignment can take? (He became a quadriplegic after a biking accident but was still able to continue his counseling practice.) What lessons can we learn from his willingness to accept this new assignment and trust in God's plans for the future?

Bible Study

1. Gideon was asked to handle a big assignment from the Lord (Judg. 6:14–16). From the following verses, what were some of the lessons he learned?

> Judges 6:22–24
> Judges 6:25–27
> Judges 6:34
> Judges 8:23

Can the lessons Gideon learned apply to a situation you are facing? If so, how?

2. Hebrews 11 introduces a wide range of people noted for their faith. Some are well-known, but many are not. A number were reluctant to follow God's

lead; most were deeply flawed individuals who found God faithful to use them in a variety of assignments.

Read Hebrews 11:32–38. You'll notice Gideon made the list even though he was fearful and had a low image of himself. Write down some of the assignments God gave to His people.

What do these descriptions tell you about the direction the Lord's purposes might take in your life? Are you prepared to handle a difficult assignment?

3. In the book of Exodus, we learn about the instructions God gave for a crucial assignment—the building of the tabernacle. He emphasized more than just creating a functional structure and items of furniture. Read the following verses to discover what else was essential to God in the design.

> Exodus 25:10–18: In constructing the ark of the covenant, what type of design was God after?
>
> Exodus 28:2, 5–6: Instead of creating ordinary garments for the priests, what were God's directions?
>
> Exodus 31:1–5: What did God do for Bezalel, and what priorities were given to him?
>
> Exodus 31:6; 38:23: Why did God choose Oholiab to help Bezalel build the tabernacle? Exodus 38:23 appears to indicate Oholiab had complementary skills (weaver of fabrics and fine linens, where Bezalel worked with metals and wood). How might that example apply to what you do for the Lord?

4. Read Exodus 31:7–11. Look at the variety of work God called Bezalel and Oholiab to do. There are at least eighteen categories covered. What does this tell you about God's vision and how He wants to use you in His service to others?

In what ways does your vision in serving the Lord need to grow?

Chapter 9: Heroic Invisibility
Discussion Questions

1. How does the concept of heroic invisibility relate to you or someone you know?

2. The value system of heaven says you are a hero when you honor your vows to God and others for life regardless of any recognition from the world. Does that change the way you think about the roles you have (spouse, parent, friend, worker) in your service to God?

Are there areas of invisibility where you could use some encouragement?

3. Do you know a hidden hero in your midst? What could you do to cheer him or her on?

Bible Study

1. The genealogies recorded in the book of 1 Chronicles are often skipped over by readers. However, they are surprisingly important, revealing how God's purposes were accomplished through the lives of a broad range of individuals. Some of the people listed were invisible to the world but highly visible to heaven.

After hundreds of names are listed with little description, the chronicler pauses on the name of Jabez. Read 1 Chronicles 4:9–10, and write out what you learn about this invisible individual.

What was it about Jabez that compelled the chronicler to raise him up as a special example in the genealogies?

Are there qualities from Jabez's life that you would like to develop in your own life? Explain.

2. The author of 1 Chronicles did not leave any clues about his identity. Why do you think he did that?

3. Read Hebrews 11:35–38, which references heroic individuals who suffered to the point of martyrdom in their commitment to God. It is interesting to note that not a single name is mentioned in these verses. Write down what the text highlights about their lives and character.

How does verse 38 describe these "invisible heroes"? Express what this means to you.

Chapter 10: Famous in Heaven
Discussion Questions

1. How does being "famous in heaven" (living for what is important in heaven rather than on the earth) apply to you in light of your current circumstances?

2. Who is in the heavenly stands cheering you on?

3. If you could place a rock on a pile of standing stones in commemoration of someone, who would you choose to honor? Explain why.

4. How would you describe the race you have been running for the Lord? Are you giving it all you have, or have you slowed to a jog or walk? What changes, if any, do you think you need to make?

Bible Study

1. Being famous in heaven shifts the priority of our earthly endeavors to what matters in God's eyes. Look at the following verses, and note what they say about seeking earthly fulfillment.

Ecclesiastes 1:14; 2:11
Psalm 103:15–16
Mark 8:36–37
1 Corinthians 3:11–15

2. Read the story of the poor widow who dropped two small copper coins into the temple treasury (Mark 12:41–44). What do you think motivated her to put in everything she owned? How was she going to survive?

Did she have any idea that her life was on display before Jesus, the Son of God, deity incarnate? In what ways was she famous in heaven?

Chapter 11: Decades, Not Days
Discussions Questions

1. How does the concept of "decades, not days" provide perspective regarding the time line God is using in your life?

What insights does Leonardo da Vinci's painting technique of adding thirty or more microlayers of glaze on the face of the *Mona Lisa* add to this idea?

2. Sometimes we think we're waiting on God when actually He might be waiting on us. Does any area of your life come to mind where this might be true?

3. Knowing that the process takes time, what aspects of your character and integrity do you think are being developed?

4. Based on what you have learned about "decades, not days," is there a step of action for you to take this week? This month?

Bible Study

1. What does the Bible emphasize about the life of Benaiah in 2 Samuel 23:20–23?

How do you think he handled not attaining the status of "three mighty men"?

Many years later, King Solomon appointed Benaiah as general over the entire army (1 Kings 2:35). What did this say about Benaiah's character and how he used his abilities during that long season of waiting?

2. Moses lived to be 120 years old. His life was divided into three forty-year segments. These lengthy time periods were used by God to prepare Moses for his unique service to the people of God in freeing them from Pharaoh's rule and leading them to the Promised Land. Describe some of the lessons Moses learned and the trials he endured during each of these phases of his life:

> Birth to 40 years old (Acts 7:20–29; Exod. 2:11–15)
> 40 to 80 years old (Acts 7:30–36; Exod. 2:15–21; 3:1–2, 10–12)
> 80 to 120 years old (Deut. 29:5–9; 30:19–20; 31:2)

Do you identify with any part of Moses's life? Are you in a season of preparation? What do you think God has in store for you? Explain.

Chapter 12: Be Ready
Discussion Questions
1. How would you answer the question posed at the beginning of this chapter: "If God was looking for someone to use on an important assignment for the kingdom, would you be the one He'd choose, given your present attitude, behavior, and choices?" Explain why or why not.

2. A hero of the faith, Peter, stumbled when his hour came. He denied knowing Jesus after being confronted by a servant girl in the court of the high priest. However, he later repented and was used greatly in God's kingdom. What does this say to you about forgiveness and the opportunity to finish well in life?

3. Is there anything in your life that needs to change so you will be ready when God's next assignment knocks on your door?

Bible Study
1. Let's learn more about Jehoshabeath ("Beth") and the type of person she was by reading 2 Chronicles 22:10–12. What descriptions and qualities of her life do these verses present?

Do you think she was aware that the hour of her larger assignment from God had arrived? Why or why not?

2. Beth's father was the evil king Jehoram. Describe how he began his rule and the kind of man he was from 2 Chronicles 21:4–6.

How did Beth's knowledge about her father's actions prepare her for the future assignment she would receive from God?

What insights about God's assignments does this give you?

3. Jehoiada ("Joe") handled his expanded assignment for the Lord while his wife, Beth, kept the future king, baby Joash, safe. You can read an overview of his life and leadership in 2 Chronicles 23:1–24:16. (See also 2 Kings 11:4–12:15.) Let's review selected examples from Joe's life and see how they challenge us about stepping out for God:

> 2 Chronicles 23:1: What were the first things Joe did when he was going to implement his plans for putting Joash on the throne?
>
> 2 Chronicles 23:7–10: What type of commitment was Joe expecting from the Levites who came to help him? What does this imply about the seriousness of Joe's attitude regarding his assignment from God? How does our commitment in serving the Lord compare?
>
> 2 Chronicles 23:16–17: After God's assignment was fulfilled and Joash was king, what were Joe's next priorities?

4. Some finishing-well verses were written about Joe in 2 Chronicles 24:15–16. Note what was emphasized about his life.

Now try writing some finishing-well verses for yourself. What qualities would you like to have in your life?

Are there any character traits you would like to strengthen in yourself? Write them down, and decide what steps of action you will take in the next thirty days to build up those areas. Watch God show up as you ask Him for help.

Chapter 13: Drink the Cup

Discussion Questions

1. Have you ever experienced a physical challenge that pushed you to the limit of your endurance? Describe.

2. Dietrich Bonhoeffer made the following statement about the German church as it remained silent in the face of the government's increasing oppression of its Jewish citizens during World War II: "It [the church] must not just bandage the victims under the wheel, but to put a spoke into the wheel itself [to stop it]." What do you think he meant by using that illustration?

Do you need to step out of your comfort zone and take action to support anyone? Explain what that person's need is.

3. The process for making coffee has similarities to the development of our spiritual maturity. If you had to describe what stage you are in or have been in, what would it be (picking, drying, hulling, roasting, grinding, brewing, or pouring out)?

4. Are you "drinking a cup" for the Lord right now or avoiding it? Explain.

If the latter, what can you do to change that?

Bible Study

1. Just a few verses in the Bible are dedicated to Zechariah, the son of Jehoiada and Jehoshabeath, but they are filled with meaning. It is clear that his father and mother imparted many significant priorities and qualities to him. What type of a man was Zechariah from what you read in 2 Chronicles 24:20?

At great personal risk, he spoke God's words to the people. How did the royal court and officials respond to what he said (2 Chron. 24:21)?

The text makes a special point emphasizing King Joash's heartless command to kill Zechariah. His father and mother had saved Joash's life and been his mentor for forty years. How could Joash forget all the kindnesses done to him by Jehoiada and Jehoshabeath?

What warning does that give us about our own hearts?

2. Read Isaiah 53:10–12, and think about all that Jesus suffered on your behalf. What does it mean to you that Jesus was crushed and experienced anguish to offer Himself for your salvation?

3. Read 1 Peter 2:21–24. The apostle Peter may have been thinking about the words of Isaiah 53 when he wrote, "For you have been called for this purpose, since Christ also suffered for you, leaving you an example for you to follow in His steps" (v. 21). Explain what this verse says to you and how it applies to your life.

Chapter 14: Faithful to the End
Discussion Questions

1. How common would you say it is for people to stay faithful to the Lord throughout their entire lives? Why do you think it is often difficult to do?

2. What stands out about the lives of Antipas and William Tyndale (pp. 197–199) that gave them the strength to remain faithful to God in the face of persecution?

3. As you look at the sculpture of Saint Cecilia (p. 200), what about her life was Stefano Maderno trying to depict?

4. Where do you need strength in order to be faithful to God in your life? Spend some time in prayer committing yourself to that important goal.

Bible Study

1. In the letters to the seven churches of Revelation, the message to Pergamum talks about the first martyr in Asia—Antipas. Read Revelation 2:12–17 and answer the following questions.

What type of culture and church environment did Antipas live in (vv. 13–15)? Note for clarification:

The teaching of Balaam—a message and lifestyle of spiritual compromise with the world (Num. 22:7–8; 31:16; 2 Pet. 2:15). Balaam was a pagan diviner who sought personal gain by charging fees for his religious work without regard to honoring God.

The Nicolaitans—a heretical sect in the church who also compromised their faith to get along with the world. They comingled pagan practices with Christianity.

In all the seven letters to the churches, Antipas was the only person identified by name for his faithfulness to Christ. From this letter to Pergamum (Rev. 2:12–17), describe why you think that was the case. What characterized Antipas?

Compare today's church in its beliefs and lifestyle with those of the believers in the church of Pergamum. Explain the similarities and the differences.

2. The apostle John was the only disciple who lived to old age, not dying a martyr's death. He wrote the book of Revelation on Patmos, a small rocky island about fifty miles southwest of Ephesus, which many believed was used as a Roman penal colony.

Read Revelation 1:9–11. How did John describe what life was like as a follower of Jesus? Why was he sentenced to Patmos (v. 9)?

What personal qualities did he demonstrate in being faithful to the end (vv. 9–11)?

Since John lived into his later years while the rest of the disciples were martyred younger, what does this communicate about the meaning of being faithful to the end?

Chapter 15: Think Differently
Discussion Questions
1. How has the fear of man affected your life? Have you missed out on anything because of it?

What were the consequences of this attitude on the nation of Israel as they stood on the border of the Promised Land the first time?

2. Just before entering the Promised Land the second time, Joshua heard the Lord speak words of courage that would become the hallmark of his life: "Every place on which the sole of your foot treads, I have given it to you, just as I spoke to Moses.... No man will be able to stand before you all the days of your life. Just as I have been with Moses, I will be with you; I will not fail you or forsake you" (Josh. 1:3, 5).

What were the important things that God wanted Joshua to know?

How do they apply to us in dealing with the mountains that confront our lives?

Do you remember any words of encouragement that someone has spoken to you before? If so, what did the person say? What impact did the encouraging words have on you?

3. This chapter introduced four kings of the Enemy that attack our minds. They were the King of Rejection, King of Fear, King of Failure, and the King of Low Self-Esteem. Do you identify with any of these kings? Explain.

Are there other kings you would add to the list that have been problems? How have they battled against you? In what ways can you draw on the truth of God's Word to defeat them?

Look at the list of lies spoken by the enemy kings on page 210. Which ones most affect you? Would you add any more?

What truth(s) from the Lord will you start telling yourself to battle against these kings?

4. Understanding the greatness of God is crucial to our spiritual victory and watching God move the mountains in our lives. Write down the descriptions of God's power over the Enemy noted on pages 213–214 that impact you. You may want to add more of your own.

5. Look at the prayer statements of God's truth presented in the sections on "'Praying Down' in Victory," page 222 and "Mirror Talk," pages 223–224. Which ones are meaningful to you? How can you make them a part of your prayer life?

6. Based on what you've learned about thinking differently, is there a step of action to take this week in response?

Bible Study

1. Joshua led the nation of Israel through many epic battles to take possession of the Promised Land. Read Joshua 10:16–27 about the five captured kings, and describe what he did to them. Does his object lesson surprise you?

What point do you think Joshua was trying to make to his commanders and soldiers? Why did he stop in the middle of their military campaign to do this?

Are there some necks of "enemy kings" that the Lord wants you to stand on in His power? Who would they be?

Is there anything holding you back from standing on them?

2. Joshua spoke encouraging words to his troops about their battle: "Don't ever be afraid or discouraged.... Be strong and courageous, for the LORD is going to do this to all of your enemies" (Josh. 10:25 NLT).

How do these words speak to you today?

Memorize this verse and repeat it daily this week, inserting your name at the beginning. Notice the exclamation points! Be sure to speak it boldly with confidence.

> [Your name:] Do not fear or be dismayed! Be strong and coura-
> geous, for thus the LORD will do to all your enemies with whom
> you fight! (Josh. 10:25)

3. How does the text in Joshua 11:18—"Joshua waged war a long time with all these kings"—apply to your personal struggles and the mountains blocking your path?

4. We read in this chapter that Joshua had to defeat thirty-one kings to take possession of the Promised Land (Josh. 12:7–24). What application from this summary can you make to your current circumstances?

Do you think you tend to give up the fight too soon in the battles you face? Why or why not? How does this impact your ability to finish well?

5. An important emphasis of the chapter was to replace our small view of God with the incredible grandeur of His qualities.

Read the following verses, and underline the characteristics of God that are emphasized. Go back through and circle those that speak to you most directly. Let these become a prayer emphasis for you this week.

> Then I saw a great white throne and Him who sat upon it, from whose presence earth and heaven fled away, and no place was found for them. (Rev. 20:11)

> Hallelujah! Salvation and glory and power belong to our God.... Hallelujah! ... Hallelujah! ... Give praise to our God, all you His bond-servants.... Hallelujah! For the Lord our God, the Almighty, reigns. (Rev. 19:1–6)

> [Jesus is] far above all rule and authority and power and dominion, and every name that is named, not only in this age but also in the one to come. And He put all things in subjection under His feet. (Eph. 1:21–22)

> But in all these things we overwhelmingly conquer through Him who loved us. For I am convinced that neither death, nor life, nor angels, nor principalities, nor things present, nor things to come, nor powers, nor height, nor depth, nor any other created thing, will be able to separate us from the love of God, which is in Christ Jesus our Lord. (Rom. 8:37–39)

Ah Lord GOD! Behold, You have made the heavens and the earth by Your great power and by Your outstretched arm! Nothing is too difficult for You … O great and mighty God. The LORD of hosts is His name; great in counsel and mighty in deed. (Jer. 32:17–19)

6. Understanding the authority we have in Christ is a crucial advantage when dealing with the Enemy of our souls. Compare Ephesians 1:20–22 and 2:5–6. Where is Jesus seated, and where are we seated?

Based on the text in Ephesians 2:6, which says we are "raised up with Him, and seated … with Him in the heavenly places," the chapter introduces the concept of "praying down" with the authority of Christ. How does this idea of praying down help us stand firm against the Enemy in our prayer lives?

7. In Ephesians 6, the apostle Paul told his readers to stand firm three times (vv. 11, 13–14). Read Ephesians 6:10–17, and identify where you need to make a stronger stand for the Lord in your life.

How does the meaning of standing firm—"standing tall in victory like a Roman soldier"— apply to the areas you have identified?

Chapter 16: The Finish
Discussion Questions

1. In Michelangelo's fresco of *The Last Judgment of Christ*, angels are holding two books pointed down to earth—a large one and a small one (see p. 229). His painting illustrates that fewer people will find salvation, filling only a small book—the Book of Life (Matt. 7:13–14; Rev. 20:12, 15). Why do you think that is the case?

2. Describe what you think it might be like to stand before God to give an account of your life. Would you be ready for that moment if it happened today? Why or why not?

3. Paul wrote, "But on the judgment day, fire will reveal what kind of work each builder has done. The fire will show if a person's work has any value. If the work survives, that builder will receive a reward. But if the work is burned up, the builder will suffer great loss. The builder will be saved, but like someone barely escaping through a wall of flames" (1 Cor. 3:13–15 NLT). Is there anything that comes to your mind that needs to be made right prior to that meeting with God? If so, what should be done?

4. Which of the three words that form the heart of a life that finishes well—*integrity*, *courage*, and *reward*—is most meaningful to you right now? Why?

5. As you look at the painting of *The Four Horsemen (Of One Spirit)* by G. Harvey, what stands out to you as it relates to finishing well?

If a painting could be made depicting your life's journey, what image would you choose?

6. Are you willing to commit yourself to finishing well for the Lord and trusting Him to move your mountains no matter what the personal cost might be? If so, sign your name here with the date:

_____

What three things will you commit to do in the next three months to pursue your decision to finish well for the Lord?

Who will you tell about it?

Bible Study

1. Read the following verse, and circle what you think is most important about the Book of Life and those whose names are in it. Explain.

> All who are victorious will be clothed in white. I will never erase
> their names from the Book of Life, but I will announce before
> my Father and his angels that they are mine. (Rev. 3:5 NLT)

2. What about those whose names are written only in the general books, not in the Book of Life? Circle what is significant in their case. Why were their names listed only in these general books?

> And all the people who belong to this world worshiped the beast. They are the ones whose names were not written in the Book of Life before the world was made—the Book that belongs to the Lamb who was slaughtered. (Rev. 13:8 NLT)

> And anyone whose name was not found recorded in the Book of Life was thrown into the lake of fire. (Rev. 20:15 NLT)

3. Paul wrote, "I have fought the good fight, I have finished the course, I have kept the faith; in the future there is laid up for me the crown of righteousness, which the Lord, the righteous Judge, will award to me on that day; and not only to me, but also to all who have loved His appearing" (2 Tim. 4:7–8). While you haven't completed your race for the Lord yet, how are you currently fighting the good fight, finishing the course, and keeping the faith?

4. Write a closing prayer (using some of Paul's words if you want) about your commitment to finish well for the Lord and to someday hear these words described about you, "Well done, good and faithful servant!"

APPENDIX A
A Personal Relationship with God

God wants to have a personal relationship with you. Look at what Psalm 139 says about His involvement in your life (vv. 1–5, 13–16 NLT):

- He knows everything about you.
- He knows when you sit down or stand up.
- He knows your thoughts.
- He knows when you travel or rest at home.
- He knows everything you do.
- He knows what you are going to say before you say it.
- He goes before you and behind you.
- He blesses you.
- He made you wonderfully complex and marvelous.
- He saw when you were born.
- He knew every day of your life before a single day had passed.

We often don't realize the love and connection God has with us each day. However, at the center of it all is a fundamental spiritual problem. We face an obstacle that prevents us from knowing God personally.

Our Situation

It may come as a surprise, but we are actually separated from God because of our sin, which includes a wide range of wrongful attitudes and behaviors. No amount of "being good" on our part can tip the scales in our favor when the standard is God's perfect holiness. In comparison to God's perfection, the prophet Isaiah said, "All our righteous deeds are like a filthy garment" (Isa. 64:6). The following verses further describe our situation:

But your iniquities have made a separation between you and your God, and your sins have hidden his face from you so that He does not hear. (Isa. 59:2)

For all have sinned and fall short of the glory of God. (Rom. 3:23)

For the wages of sin is death. (Rom. 6:23)

God's Solution

It is impossible to resolve the problem of our separation from God through our own efforts. He alone has the power to provide the solution for us. He did that by taking the punishment for our sins on Himself through the sacrifice of Jesus Christ on the cross. Jesus defeated death's grip by rising again to life. The Bible describes it in this way:

For God so loved the world, that He gave His only begotten Son, that whoever believes in Him shall not perish, but have eternal life. (John 3:16)

And there is salvation in no one else; for there is no other name under heaven that has been given among men by which we must be saved. (Acts 4:12)

But God demonstrates His own love toward us, in that while we were yet sinners, Christ died for us. (Rom. 5:8)

Having been justified by faith, we have peace with God through our Lord Jesus Christ. (Rom. 5:1)

For there is one God and one Mediator who can reconcile God and humanity—the man Christ Jesus. He gave his life to purchase freedom for everyone. (1 Tim. 2:5–6 NLT)

Our Response

We are invited by God to respond to all that He has done for us by receiving Jesus Christ as our Savior. We come to God on His terms, not our own. The Bible teaches that the way of salvation is through Jesus Christ alone.

> Jesus said to him, "I am the way, and the truth, and the life; no one comes to the Father but through Me." (John 14:6)

> Jesus said to her, "I am the resurrection and the life; he who believes in Me will live even if he dies, and everyone who lives and believes in Me will never die. Do you believe this?" (John 11:25–26)

We receive Jesus Christ by faith. It is often expressed in prayer with heartfelt words that we believe in Jesus as our Savior and want to follow Him as the Lord of our life. The words may vary, but they acknowledge that we are separated from God and that we can't save ourselves.

A simple prayer could go like this:

Dear Lord Jesus,

I know that I am a sinner and cannot save myself. I need forgiveness for my sins—those attitudes and actions that have separated me from God. Thank You for dying on the cross and taking the punishment for sin on my behalf. You rose again and triumphed over death.

Because of what You have done, my sins are forgiven and I can have eternal life in heaven. I invite You to come into my life to be my Savior. I turn away from my old ways and will follow You now as my Lord.

In Your name I pray, amen.

If this was your prayer, you received what the Bible promises as the free gift of eternal life in Jesus Christ. It is a simple, yet profound, step of faith that you took, placing all your hope in Jesus. People for millennia have made that same decision with life-changing results.

The Bible says that there are crowds cheering in heaven whenever someone chooses to follow Christ. It is the most important decision anyone can make in life. There may be people you know who will also cheer when they hear this news. Plan a time to contact them this week to share about your new faith in Jesus Christ.

Our Assurance of Salvation

We can be certain that we are His because our salvation is founded on the promises given in God's Word. There are many verses that indicate this; here are a few:

> For "Whoever will call upon the name of the Lord will be saved." (Rom. 10:13)

> These things I have written to you who believe in the name of the Son of God, so that you may know that you have eternal life. (1 John 5:13)

> But to all who believed him and accepted him, he gave the right to become children of God. (John 1:12 NLT)

> And the testimony is this, that God has given us eternal life, and this life is in His Son. He who has the Son has the life; he who does not have the Son of God does not have the life. (1 John 5:11–12)

> The one who comes to Me I will certainly not cast out … For this is the will of My Father, that everyone who beholds the Son and believes in Him will have eternal life and I Myself will raise him up on the last day. (John 6:37, 40)

As you have committed yourself to follow Jesus Christ, an exciting new journey with the Lord is beginning. The following recommendations will help you grow in your relationship with Him:

1. Read your Bible every day if possible. It will help you grow closer to God and to know Him. A good place to start is in the New Testament with the gospel of John.

2. Make prayer a part of your daily routine. You can talk to God at home, in your car, or anywhere else. He is ready to listen and won't be offended by anything you might have to say. Since prayer is a conversation, be attentive to how He communicates back!

3. Find a good church that believes the Bible is the inspired Word of God.

4. Make friends with others who are followers of Jesus so that you can encourage one another in the faith.

5. Begin finding ways to serve the Lord and share about Him with others. As you see the Holy Spirit work through you, it will build your faith.

6. Submit every part of your life to Jesus, and watch Him work in and through you in the future.

Remember, in your new relationship with Jesus, you are the best of friends now (John 15:14)!

APPENDIX B
Book Summary

Finish-Well Definition: To finish life in right relationship to my God, spouse, family, fellow man, and the work He gave me to do.

Three Defining Words:

> *Integrity*—Honoring my vows to the Lord and to others for life
>
> *Courage*—Resolving to do whatever it takes to live with integrity
>
> *Reward*—Experiencing the benefits that come from living with integrity and courage

Daily Attitude: To be a hope-filled, yielded, determined influencer for God and His purposes in the world.

God: God wants a personal relationship with us. He cares deeply about our lives. Having a right relationship with Him is crucial for a life to finish well.

Spouse: The marriage vow is the most important next to our commitment to Jesus Christ. Don't give up on it! Leave your spouse to God and work on your own heart. Allow God to show up and be true to His name, the "Lord of the Breakthrough" (see 2 Sam. 5:20).

Family: Don't underestimate the influence of your life! It can have a multigenerational impact.

Fellow Man: Be willing to take a risk with the people God puts in your path. He will use that occasion to point them in His direction.

Work: We have many assignments from the Lord to accomplish during our lives. We rob God of His glory if we attempt only assignments that can be accomplished in our own strength.

Heroic Invisibility: Honoring our vows to the Lord regardless of any recognition from the world.

Famous in Heaven: Living according to the standards of heaven as opposed to those endorsed on the earth.

Decades, Not Days: Accepting the season of preparation that God uses to develop us for His future assignments, which often takes longer than expected.

Be Ready: Being ready in our attitude, behavior, and choices to handle God's assignment when it arrives.

Drink the Cup: Taking action to fulfill God's assignment even though it comes at great personal sacrifice.

Faithful to the End: Maintaining an uncompromising attitude that nothing will deter us from following the Lord until our last breath is taken on the earth.

Think Differently: Renewing our minds by the power of God's Word to defeat the Enemy's lies, freeing ourselves to live fully for Him.

The Finish: Standing before the Lord someday and hearing Him say, "Well done, good and faithful servant!"

APPENDIX C
Finishing Well Wheel

The following diagram shows how the priorities and principles of the book connect to one another.

The small, center triangle emphasizes that our relationship with God is at the very core of all that we do. It is surrounded by four sections, which together form the five priorities for a life that finishes well and watches God move mountains.

The next ring highlights the six principles for moving mountains that support our pursuit to finish well. They are heroic invisibility; famous in heaven; decades, not days; be ready; drink the cup; and faithful to the end.

The six qualities listed in the outer ring undergird the others. Integrity, courage, and reward capture the heart of our journey; and thinking differently, relentless pursuit, and determined influencer for God are the attitudes we need.

All together they describe a life that believes the best is yet to be, watches God move our mountains, and finishes well for Him.

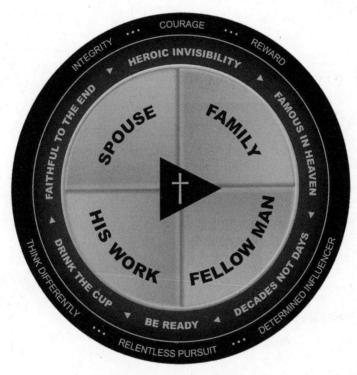

Finishing well wheel (copyright Bruce Peppin)

NOTES

Chapter 1: Life in Review

1. Mark Twain, *Autobiography of Mark Twain*, vol. 1 (Oakland, CA: University of California Press, 2010), 325–26.

2. *Mother Teresa: Come Be My Light*, ed. Brian Kolodiejchuk (New York: Doubleday, 2007), 210–11.

3. D'Vera Cohn and Paul Taylor, "Baby Boomers Approach 65—Glumly," PewSocialTrends.Org, December 20, 2010, www.pewsocialtrends. org/2010/12/20/baby-boomers-approach-65-glumly/.

Chapter 2: The Narrow Way

1. "Mother Teresa Voted by American People as Most Admired Person of the Century," Gallup, December 31, 1999, www.gallup.com/poll/3367/Mother-Teresa-Voted-American-People-Most-Admired-Person-Century.aspx.

2. *NLT Study Bible*, New Living Translation, 2nd ed. (Carol Stream, IL: Tyndale, 2008), 1624.

Chapter 3: High Risk

1. Susan Gregory Thomas, "The Gray Divorcés," *Wall Street Journal*, March 3, 2012, http://online.wsj.com/news/articles/SB100014240529702037537045772 55230471480276.

2. Howard Dayton, *Your Money Map* (Chicago: Moody, 2009).

3. Dominique François, *Normandy: Breaching the Atlantic Wall from D-Day to the Breakout and Liberation* (Minneapolis: Zenith, 2008), 69.

4. Walter Ehlers, "Medal of Honor: Lessons on Personal Bravery and Self-Sacrifice Symposium" (speech, Ronald Reagan Presidential Library, Simi Valley, CA, February 24, 2012).

5. Winston S. Churchill (Curtis Brown, London, on behalf of the Estate of Sir Winston Churchill, Copyright © Winston S. Churchill, used with permission).

Chapter 4: Going Deeper

1. John Eldredge, Ransomed Heart Ministries newsletter, September 2007.

2. Ann Voskamp, *One Thousand Gifts: A Dare to Live Fully Right Where You Are* (Grand Rapids, MI: Zondervan, 2010), 44.

3. John and Joanna Stumbo, *An Honest Look at a Mysterious Journey* (Chippewa Falls, WI: Nesting Tree Books, 2011), 31.

4. C. S. Lewis, *The Last Battle* (New York: HarperCollins, 1994), 167–69.

5. William F. Graham Jr., *Nearing Home: Life, Faith, and Finishing Well* (Nashville: Thomas Nelson, 2011), 168.

6. C. S. Lewis, *The Weight of Glory and Other Addresses* (San Francisco: HarperSanFrancisco, 2001), 26.

Chapter 5: Mr. and Mrs.

1. Brennan Manning, *The Furious Longing of God* (Colorado Springs: David C Cook, 2009), 35.

2. Brian Mansfield, "Premiere: Casting Crowns' 'Broken Together'" *USA Today*, January 20, 2014, www.usatoday.com/story/life/music/2014/01/20/casting-crowns-broken-together-premiere/4653079/.

Chapter 6: Pebble or Boulder

1. Robin Donica Wolaver, *The Song of Annie Moses: A Musical Quest, a Mother's Gift* (New York: Guideposts, 2013).

2. Martin Luther (1483–1546), "A Mighty Fortress Is Our God."

3. Special thanks to Ray Vander Laan for the insights shared in this section about Abraham and the tamarisk tree from *Walking with God in the Desert* DVD and *Discovery Guide* (Colorado Springs: Focus on the Family, 2010).

4. Vander Laan, *Walking*, 139–40.

5. Vander Laan, *Walking*, 138.

Chapter 7: Unexpected Friends

1. Peggy Noonan, "Faces of Love," *Wall Street Journal*, March 11, 2003.

Chapter 8: Assignments

1. Comments based on Mark Batterson, *In a Pit with a Lion on a Snowy Day: How to Survive and Thrive When Opportunity Roars* (Colorado Springs: Multnomah, 2006).

2. Dr. Joe Wheeler, letter to author, January 7, 2007.

Chapter 12: Be Ready

1. Alison Levine, *On the Edge: The Art of High-Impact Leadership* (New York: Hachette, 2014), 2–3.

2. Winston S. Churchill (Curtis Brown, London, on behalf of the Estate of Sir Winston Churchill, Copyright © Winston S. Churchill, used with permission).

Chapter 13: Drink the Cup

1. Eric Metaxas, *Bonhoeffer: A Biography* (Nashville: Thomas Nelson, 2010), 154.
2. Metaxas, *Bonhoeffer*, 494–95.
3. Metaxas, *Bonhoeffer*, 495.
4. Metaxas, *Bonhoeffer*, 528.
5. The reference to Zechariah in Matthew 23:35 states that Berechiah was his father where 2 Chronicles 24:20 and 24:22 say that Jehoiada was. Commentators believe he was probably the grandson of Jehoiada the priest, noting that Old Testament genealogies sometimes left out unimportant names in order to connect an individual to a famous ancestor. This appears to be the case here. We are using the designation of Jehoiada as Zechariah's father based on the text in 2 Chronicles.

Chapter 14: Faithful to the End

1. Kenneth L. Barker, ed., et al., "Study Notes on Revelation," *Zondervan NASB Study Bible* (Grand Rapids, MI: Zondervan, 1999), 1851.
2. This section is enhanced by personal trip notes the author took while in Pergamum during Ray Vander Laan's That the World May Know study tour of the seven churches of Revelation, Turkey, September 2005.
3. Stefano Maderno claimed that his sculpture accurately depicted the position of Cecilia's body when her tomb was opened in 1599. Opinions vary regarding the certainty of the description.

Chapter 15: Think Differently

1. Rick Renner, *Spiritual Weapons to Defeat the Enemy: Overcoming the Wiles, Devices, and Deception of the Devil* (Tulsa, OK: Teach All Nations, 2012), 39, 57.
2. Renner, *Spiritual Weapons*, 71.
3. John Maxwell, *How Successful People Think* (New York: Hachette, 2009), 123.

Chapter 16: The Finish

1. Marcia Hall, *Michelangelo: The Frescoes of the Sistine Chapel* (New York: Harry N. Abrams, 2002), 216.
2. Randy Alcorn, *The Treasure Principle* (Colorado Springs: Multnomah, 2001), 48–49.
3. Andy Andrews, *The Butterfly Effect: How Your Life Matters* (Nashville: Thomas Nelson, 2009), 102–9.
4. "Introduction to the Second Letter of Paul to Timothy," *The Ryrie Study Bible*, New American Standard Version (Chicago: Moody, 1978), 1823.

CONTACT THE AUTHOR

To connect with Bruce, visit his website at www.brucepeppin.com.

Bruce is available to speak on the topics presented in this book and what it means to finish well for the Lord. For more information, refer to the website above.